Poverty

Rodopi Philosophical Studies

6

Edited by
Francisco Miró Quesada
(University of Lima)

Ernest Sosa
(Brown University)

Amsterdam - New York, NY 2005

Poverty

A Philosophical Approach

Paulette Dieterlen

The paper on which this book is printed meets the requirements of "ISO 9706:1994, Information and documentation - Paper for documents - Requirements for permanence".

ISBN: 90-420-1975-1
Editions Rodopi B.V ., Amsterdam - New York, NY 2005
Printed in the Netherlands

For Emilio, Alejandro and Maurizio

CONTENTS

FOREWORD

The idea of writing a book about poverty arose after having studied over a long period the main aspects of the theory of justice. Obviously, Rawls's *A Theory of Justice* was a major influence. My interest in concentrating on a particular aspect of justice arose from the reading of Michael Walzer and Jon Elster. It was Amartya Sen who led me directly to the subject of poverty.

I have discussed my work in many academic forums and been greatly stimulated by the exchange of ideas with colleagues. Among these I would like to mention Elisabetta Di Castro, to whom I am particularly grateful; I must point out that in recent years all my texts have passed before her acute and intelligent gaze. Discussions in the Program for Advanced Studies in Sustainable Development and Environment at El Colegio de México were for me extremely enriching, and what I learned from Boris Graizbord, Rosa María Ruvalcaba, Fernando Cortés and Enrique Hernández Laos was decisive. My gratitude is due to Alicia Ziccardi for the invitation to take part in the Forum on Poverty organized by the CLACSO working group. Julio Boltvinik showed interest in my work and provided me with material related to the so-called and much discussed "poverty lines".

I had the opportunity to spend a sabbatical year in the Mexican Government's Education, Health and Food Program (PROGRESA), thanks to the generosity and interest shown in the subject of my research by the Program's coordinator at the time, José Gómez de León. To a large extent this book is due to him. In Mexico, any person who takes seriously the study and application of policies to combat poverty must inevitably have in mind a memory of "Pepe". Many people helped me at PROGRESA, among them Magdalena Torres, Susan Parker, Patricia Muñoz and Daniel Hernández.

Several of the ideas expressed here can be found in articles and chapters of books published beforehand;[1] I should like to express my

---

[1] "PROGRESA y la atención a las necesidades básicas", in *Alivio a la pobreza, análisis de del Programa de Educación, Salud y Alimentación*, CIESAS and PROGRESA, Mexico City, 1998, pp. 130–143; with José Gómez de León, "Diversidad humana, libertad y capacidades en la obra de Amartya Sen", *Metapolítica*, no. 10, vol. 3, April-June, 1999, pp. 339–351; "Dos conceptos de pobreza", in Juliana González (ed.), *Moral y poder*, Secretaría de Educación Pública/Academia Mexicana de Ciencias y Tecnología/Consejo Consultivo de Ciencias de la Presidencia de la República,

thanks to the editors of the works in which these texts appeared. I also wish to thank María Dolores de la Peña, who carried out the first revision of the work, and, of course, the Editorial Committee of the Instituto de Investigaciones Filosóficas of the UNAM in Mexico City which sent the original Spanish version of this book to the adjudicators, who made extremely valuable comments. Thanks are also due to the Head of the Institute's Publications Department, Carolina Celorio, and to its editors Laura Manríquez, Claudia Chávez and José Alberto Barrañón for the effort they invested in preparing the book for publication; likewise to Adolfo Castañón, Jesús Guerrero and Luis Valverde at the Fondo de Cultura Económica. I would like to mention that the book was one of the final outcomes of a project entitled *Filosofía política y racionalidad* (PAPIIT IN400598). The support I received from the General Directorate of Assistance to Academic Staff at the Universidad NacionalAutónoma de México was fundamental. My thanks are also due to Andrés Moles and Luis Enrique Camacho, excellent philosophy students who helped me with great generosity to revise the work.

Finally, my most sincere gratitude to Ariel Zúñiga: his enthusiasm and his generosity made it possible for his father's lithograph to appear on the book's cover.

It is worth mentioning that on March 15, 2002, the agreement setting forth the rules of operation for the human development program "Oportunidades" (which replaced PROGRESA) appeared in the pages of the Mexican Government's official gazette (*Diario Oficial de la Federación*). The new program aims to give a broader coverage; support is not only provided in rural areas but also to the urban population. It also includes assistance for pupils at the pre-university level. It is also significant that on August 13, 2002, the Federal Gov-

---

Mexico City, 2000, pp. 91–98; "Algunos aspectos filosóficos del Programa de Educación, Salud y Alimentación", *Estudios sociológicos*, vol. XVIII, no. 52, January-April, 2000, pp. 191–202; "Democracia, pobreza y exclusión", in Luis Villoro (ed.), *Perspectivas de la democracia en México*, El Colegio de México, 2001, pp. 121–174; "Some Philosophical Considerations on Mexico's Educational, Health and Food Program", in Arleen L.F. Salles and María Julia Bertomeu (eds.), *Bioethics, Latin American Perspectives*, Rodopi, Amsterdam/New York, 2001, pp. 85–106; "Derechos, necesidades básicas y obligación institucional", in Alicia Ziccardi (comp.), *Pobreza, desigualdad social ciudadanía. Los límites de las políticas sociales en América Latina*, CLACSO, Buenos Aires, 2001, pp. 13–22.

ernment announced the introduction of three different categories for measuring poverty in Mexico. These are: "food poverty", which includes Mexicans with a daily income of less than 20 pesos in the cities, or 15 pesos in the countryside, which is insufficient even to provide a minimum of food; "capabilities poverty", which takes in those earning 24 pesos in urban areas and 18 in rural zones; and finally "patrimony poverty", which includes those earning up to 41 pesos in towns and cities, and up to 28 in the countryside.[2]

---

[2] See Cecilia González, "Pretenden garantizar mínimo de bienestar", *Reforma*, Mexico City, August 14, 2002. p 6A.

INTRODUCTION

One of the leading problems with which political philosophy has struggled throughout its history is that of the rights of individuals *vis-à-vis* the state and other citizens. Foremost in this debate were John Locke and John Stuart Mill. Rights themselves were the source of great polemics like the one that took place between advocates of natural law and defenders of the concept of positive law. There is no doubting the importance, as a source of general concern, of questions concerning the use of power, its legitimacy or what serves to legitimate it; how the mechanisms of power operate in societies, its recourse to "hidden springs", as Foucault would have it, or to "transparent" mechanisms such as rewards and punishments. In recent times numerous studies of systems of government have appeared, among which the concern for democracy—examined from the point of view of systems of representation and the question of who is included in decision-making processes—is paramount. Likewise the role played by the "checks and balances" of political decision-making in democracies has been extensively studied, with particular attention to the weight of individual rights in the face of decisions taken by majority vote, and the implications of the separation of powers.

Another all-important question has been that of the boundaries between public and private realms; this is, perhaps, the question that liberal thought has been most concerned to submit to discussion. One which have recurred throughout the history of political thought is, of course, that of exclusion and inclusion—in other words the question of the rules of play that allow us to identify who are *inside* and those who are barred from decision-making in politics. For instance, in classical Greece, the excluded were slaves, women and the foreign settlers or *metoikoi*. This situation has obviously changed throughout history; nevertheless, the subject of exclusion is still a matter that demands our attention. At present, in a democratic state like Mexico, it can fairly be stated that the excluded are the poor. I believe, however, that the question of poverty has been overlooked in many discussions in the field of political philosophy. This is so for a number of reasons, among which is the fact that the poor do not constitute, in general, a political force that claims the attention of political philosophers, nor even, perhaps, of the media. Of Mexico's 96 million inhabitants, some 40 million live in a situation of poverty and 27 million in extreme poverty, which is reason enough for feeling obliged to take them into account. In democracies the excluded are the poor, and thus a philosophical reflection upon poverty is urgently needed. When we pause to think about poverty, we encounter a number of questions that are characteristic not only of political philosophy but also of ethics. Also, given the diversity of places and cultures where the victims of extreme poverty are to be found, it is difficult to deal with them as a single object of reflection. Poverty has been studied mainly by sociologists, anthropologists, economists and demographers, but very little by philosophers.

In recent years, however, interest in studying poverty has increased among practitioners of this discipline. This is no doubt a consequence of the publication in 1971 of John Rawls's *A Theory of Justice*, which set the problem of equitable distribution and the need to harmonize certain apparently incompatible principles, such as freedom and equality, in the center of discussion. Likewise, some economists—specifically those known as "developmentalists", such as Amartya Sen and Partha Dasgupta—began to contribute ideas to the philosophical debate. This debate has taken place in a framework defined by what at present is called "distributive justice". This has two aspects: first, there is the theoretical discussion; secondly, practical application, in so far as such theorizing contributes to design policies to combat poverty.

Distributive justice comprises several elements. A matter of considerable importance is the conception decision makers have of the subjects eligible to receive assistance in the form of goods or services; as we shall see further on, if the poor are regarded as passive beings, ignorant of their needs and incapable of choosing what is best for them, paternalistic policies will be implemented. On the contrary, if they are regarded as agents in their own right, policies will be designed to help them form their own life plans.

Another important matter concerns what is selected for distribution. Some items may be thought of as satisfiers of people's basic needs, others are "enabling" items that help them give expression to their preferences. Surely the progression from a general concept of the good as "what every rational man desires" (as mentioned by Rawls) to that of specific goods that have a shared social meaning—

as developed by Walzer in *Spheres of Justice* or by Elster in *Local Justice*—is highly significant.

Finally, we meet the argument which, from my point of view, constitutes the nucleus of distributive justice: the criteria of distribution, in other words what, in Robert Nozick's words, ought to fill in the gap in the phrase "to each according to his...". The criteria of distribution are indispensable, particularly when considering public policies, since these have to be planned against a background of scarcity of goods and services. When dealing with poverty, the consequences of such scarcity can be tragic, since the application of one criterion or another means excluding certain people from the benefits of policies, and thus depriving them of goods and services that are indispensable for them to live a human life. Likewise, scarcity leads us to make decisions that, in Guido Calabresi's and Philip Bobbit's words are, of necessity, not the best alternative, but the least bad one. These tragic decisions have real consequences for the lives of human beings.

Chapter One of this book aims to analyze what I have labeled two concepts of poverty. While it seems to me that to be poor means to be deprived of specific economic resources, it often also means to lack what several authors have referred to as self-esteem or self-respect. I examine the accounts that various economists have given of poverty and the stipulations of some philosophers regarding the conditions that a person must enjoy if she is to be considered worthy of being taken into account. I also mention some theses that deny outright the need for any struggle against poverty. While I do not share this opinion, it seems to me important to consider it. As far as the economic aspects are concerned, one point ought to be clarified: the reader should not expect the concepts of poverty that I have called economic to be accompanied by quantitative measurements or functions of utility. Some excellent studies of poverty have been carried out from an economic, demographic and sociological point of view. In Mexico there has been some extremely important research into different ways of measuring poverty. My own interest lies, however, in explaining certain ideas that arise when we speak about poverty, in particular when we refer to extreme poverty. These ideas spring from analysis carried out by economists. Another important part of this chapter involves the study of human dignity and examines arguments that have been put forward in defense of this concept.

It is at this point that what I have called the ethical conception of poverty comes in. For reasons that I shall mention towards the end of this introduction, while the matters dealt with in the different chapters refer to characteristics and problems of poverty in general, the example I choose for illustration refers exclusively to a rural sector, due to the fact that the Program which I studied only concerned this sector.

Chapter Two deals with the various criteria for distribution. This question is possibly the most interesting for a philosopher who is interested in the study of poverty. A number of positions exist defining what is of relevance for implementing a public policy, and this chapter addresses a number of different criteria: primary goods, preferences, needs, capabilities, and the mixed principles of distribution. The principle one chooses to apply is no merely theoretical matter; it is also a political decision which, as I have already mentioned, may have tragic implications. The distribution criteria are also significant in philosophy since they set out from particular conceptions of human beings that appear in some classics of this discipline.

Given that, when talking about poverty, it is common to refer to rights, Chapter Three analyzes certain positions that attack or defend the so-called welfare rights. It is important to take these into account in a study of poverty, since such rights may be essential for poor people to escape from their situation; the right to health, for instance. Social rights represent a very broad area of debate; I have thus limited myself to examining positions that directly relate to assistance to the poor. I also refer to the obligations that the rest of society should assume towards them. This chapter sets forth a concept of citizenship that involves rights and obligations, but also virtuous behavior. It seems to me that the subject of rights and obligations towards the poor is an incitement to reflection on the responsibility we as citizens have to help combat extreme poverty.

As the commonest practice for measuring poverty is the application of the principle of utility, Chapter Four aims to explain how this concept has operated in the interpretation of poverty. The idea of man as a maximizer of utility has permeated many discussions of poverty. Nonetheless, there are authors who believe that, while it may be true that in certain circumstances human beings act with the purpose of maximizing utility, in others they follow norms. This means that much of our behavior can be explained in reference to the commitments we undertake towards other members of the group and that such behavior often does not represent a maximization of utility. This matter is of tremendous importance in countries where social norms exercise a considerable pressure upon behavior. Now, it is necessary to make another clarification: while the subject of the following of norms may lead us to treat poverty from a community point of view, that discussion does not enter into the subject matter of this book. One can hardly ignore the fact that at present an important debate is taking place between liberalism and communitarianism; I should, however, stress that the idea that guided my work on this book can best be described as a liberal theory which takes the idea of equality very seriously. The reason for not entering into the above-mentioned debate is that up to the present time practically all public policies for combating poverty have been implemented taking individuals or their families into account; specific aspects of the cultures to which they might belong have not been considered.

It is the final chapter which looks into the "background" of the discussion, in other words the study of a certain type of liberal thought that tries to explain the importance of the idea of equality. Practically all the questions dealt with in the first four chapters point towards the achievement of a lesser degree of social inequality. Equality, therefore, deserved a special treatment.

Finally, I should like to stress the importance for me of introducing an example of a social policy in action. I wished thus to show that the philosophical approach is capable of bringing greater understanding to bear upon public policies and that philosophical concepts are not just abstract ideas that have nothing to do with reality.

I chose PROGRESA (the Mexican government's education, health and food program) for two reasons. The first is that in 1998 I spent a sabbatical year studying and observing the functioning of this program. Not only did I have the opportunity to become familiar with it at the theoretical level, but was also able to carry out some field trips and talk to beneficiaries of the program in the workshops organized by PROGRESA in rural areas within the jurisdiction of Mexico City; what I learned substantially modified my interests regarding poverty. The second reason is that PROGRESA has been one of the few programs set up to combat extreme poverty that have been evaluated during application. The various studies arising from this process of evaluation are an enormous aid to appreciating both the results and the problems of the program.[1]

I hope this example may serve to explain the choice of topics that make up this book. My intention is quite modest, I have merely attempted to offer for the reader's consideration a range of topics that have been discussed by philosophers concerning one of the most tragic of social, economic and political problems: poverty.

---

[1] Three documents exist: *Alivio a la pobreza. Análisis del Programa de Educación, Salud y Alimentación dentro de la política social*, published in 1998 by PROGRESA and the CIESAS; *Más oportunidades para las familias pobres (Primeros avances)*, published by PROGRESA in 1999; and the broad study, *Más oportunidades para las familias pobres*, which PROGRESA published in the year 2000.

I

TWO CONCEPTS OF POVERTY

> El mundo está detenido ante el hambre que asola a los pueblos. Mientras haya desequilibrio económico, el mundo no piensa. Yo lo tengo visto. Van dos hombres por la orilla de un río. Uno es rico, otro es pobre. Uno lleva la barriga llena, y el otro pone sucio al aire con sus bostezos. Y el rico dice: ¡Oh, qué barca más linda se ve por el agua! Mire, mire usted, el lirio florece en la orilla". Y el pobre reza: "Tengo hambre, no veo nada". Natural. El día que el hambre desaparezca, va a producirse en el mundo la explosión espiritual más grande que jamás conoció la humanidad. Nunca jamás se podrán figurar los hombres la alegría que estallará el día de la Gran Revolución.
>
> Federico García Lorca[1]

INTRODUCTION

This chapter considers two dimensions of poverty: the economic and the ethical dimensions. The economic dimension—which is dealt with from a conceptual rather than a quantitative point of view— entails an examination of some of the problems that poverty gives rise to for society as a whole and also of the consequences for those people who lack the basic elements for leading a decent human existence. Some of the arguments that have been advanced in favor of combating poverty are outlined, along with criticisms that have been made of them; some important concepts for the study of poverty are

---

[1] "The world stands still before the hunger that assails peoples. As long as the world is economically unbalanced, it doesn't think. I can picture it clearly. Two men are walking by the side of a river. One is rich, the other is poor. One has a full belly, the other makes the air filthy with his yawning. And the rich man says: 'Oh what a pretty boat is that on the river! Just look how the lily flowers at the water's edge'. And the poor man exclaims: 'I'm hungry. I don't see anything'. It's natural. The day hunger disappears, the world is going to witness the greatest explosion of spirituality mankind has ever known. Never will men be able to imagine the joy that will explode the day of the Great Revolution." Quoted by J. Riechman in "Necesidades: algunas delimitaciones en las que acaso podríamos convenir", p. 38.

also analyzed. The remaining chapters of this book are devoted to the ethical dimension, which entails formulation of the principles that ought to commit us to a serious attempt at combating poverty.

In search of a starting point for this discussion of the problem of poverty we might do well to travel back in time to the introduction of the Poor Law in Tudor England. Several reasons have been offered for this first attempt at combating poverty via an official policy. Matthew Hale, writing in the mid seventeenth century, explained the introduction of the legislation to fight poverty in terms of the increasing number of poor that appeared as a result of the country becoming "more populous".[2] Paul Slack calls this the "high-pressure" interpretation: the laws for combating poverty were a response to economic circumstances and particularly to population pressure. A second interpretation puts the accent on changes in public attitudes, the crucial factor being "a new conception of what governments could and should do for the poor, inspired by humanism, Protestantism or Puritanism (the choice varies between historians)". The third interpretation is that the initiative came from within government itself: "the political ambitions of central government, Parliament or local elites [...] who wished to control their subjects and inferiors".[3]

The argument over the State's obligation to help indigent families and the reasons for doing so continued in Great Britain, in spite of the criticisms posed by great economists such as Adam Smith and John Stuart Mill regarding the limitations of the State's intervention in the economy. Both Smith and Mill condemned certain types of State intervention in economic matters; nonetheless, they believed that poverty ought to be fought, albeit through the agency of private associations. Also influential were the powerful theses of Mandeville regarding the way in which private vices, especially pride and avarice, became public virtues redounding to the good of the economy. Notwithstanding, some thinkers saw the need for governments to act to reduce poverty. For example, 1834 saw the passing of a new Poor Law, based on the principle of "least eligibility". This meant a notable improvement in working conditions in the factories with the aim of making an honest day's work "more eligible" than a life of crime.[4]

---

[2] Cited in Paul Slack, *The English Poor Law, 1531–1782*, p. 3.
[3] Ibid.
[4] See Anthony Skillen, "Welfare State versus Welfare Society?", p. 207.

In 1869 T. H. Green, the "grandfather" of social work in Great Britain founded the Charity Organization Society. The work carried out by that society included the "scientific" study of poverty, which consisted in developing techniques for distinguishing the "deserving poor" (i.e. those who deserved help) from those who were regarded as merely the dregs of society. Green was a liberal and thus believed that it was society, rather than governments, that ought to concern itself with poverty; nevertheless, he detected significant shortcomings in the conditions of hire which led to hungry workers being obliged to accept disadvantageous agreements with the exploitative bosses.[5]

The argument in Great Britain over the role of the State in the struggle against poverty has continued even since the establishment, in 1942, of the Beveridge plan.[6] This plan was founded upon two principles. The first consisted in promoting policies that would serve all citizens and not merely sectoral interests. The second was that the British National Insurance Scheme was to be "part only of a comprehensive policy of social progress".[7] The virtues or defects of the plan are still being widely discussed.

During the 1970s, the most important studies of poverty were carried out, according to Julio Boltvinik, in Latin America, and particularly Mexico; here the UNECLA carried out which has been seen as a pioneering investigation. This work presents calculations of the incidence of poverty and of what is referred to as extreme poverty, as well as their degrees of intensity.[8] Between 1979 and 1982, research was carried out into basic needs, and an approach to poverty was developed which consisted in positing the need to establish a complete *Normative Shopping-Basket on Essential Satisfiers*. The results of this research were published by Siglo XXI and COPLAMAR. From 1986 on, the *Regional Project for Overcoming Poverty*, coordinated by Julio Boltvinik, reached an agreement with the Mexican Economic Programming and Budgeting Ministry and a working group was set up to develop a diagnosis of poverty in this country. So far, a

---

[5] Ibid., p. 208.
[6] See, for example, A.B. Atkinson. "Promise and Performance: Why We Need an Official Poverty Report", pp. 123–141.
[7] A. Skillen, op. cit., p. 202.
[8] See Julio Boltvinik, "El conocimiento de la pobreza en México", p. 81.

number of attempts have been made to carry out empirical studies of poverty.[9]

In 1977, the Mexican Government set up an agency known as COPLAMAR to apply programs to combat poverty. These were aimed at marginalized groups and deprived zones, particularly in rural areas. As Rolando Cordera reports:

> COPLAMAR is a short-run program which, nonetheless, facilitates a solid knowledge of the problem of poverty and marginalization. The notion of essential needs is not merely public and official terminology; it is [something that is] also extensively documented in the form of shortfalls and deficits in access to basic services, elementary items of consumption, etc.[10]

Cordera also provides information regarding the Mexican Food System, which aimed "to enshrine the idea of food self-sufficiency in the country's statutory framework, an urgent need brought into existence by the historical circumstances which the international petroleum crisis opened up for Mexico and the world."[11] These programs were abandoned between 1982 and 1988. Other programs for combating poverty were, however, introduced by Carlos Salinas de Gortari's administration between 1988 and 1994 in the form of "Solidaridad".[12] This program sought to respond to the accumulated demands for attention of rural and urban communities, and set out on the basis of the more or less explicit recognition that poverty was becoming a political problem.[13] Finally, with PROGRESA, introduced by Ernesto Zedillo in 1997, the governmental struggle against poverty was relaunched.

ARGUMENTS AGAINST THE WAR ON POVERTY

It seems important to emphasize that, despite the above-mentioned attention given to the study of poverty in academic political science departments and by those government institutions responsible for implementing policies for combating it, arguments have also been

---

[9] Ibid., p. 82.
[10] R. Codera. "PROGRESA y la experiencia mexicana contra la pobreza, pp. 17–18.
[11] Ibid., p. 18.
[12] Ibid., p. 11.
[13] Ibid., p. 18.

proposed which reject the idea that poverty is an ill that must be eradicated. Let us consider a few examples.

In 1970, a current of thought known as neo-Malthusianism came into view. Neo-Malthusians regard poverty as a natural disaster impossible to avoid. They offer metaphors in the form of images of uncontrollable catastrophe. Human population growth is a "time bomb"; the developed world is presented as a "life boat" that can only take on board a few more passengers without risking the lives of those already aboard. Planet Earth's capacity to withstand the weight of so many human beings is finite, and will be damaged if excessively overburdened. In the same way as with animal populations, once the human population has expanded to fill all possible ecological niches, hunger will inevitably constitute a form of natural selection. Such neo-Malthusian theses consider poverty to be both a natural disaster and one without remedy. Attempts to reduce it are pointless and counterproductive. These theses suggest that the intervention of modern technology may cause some problems to be ameliorated, but can in no way offer a solution. Actions of this type, in the form of public policies at both local and international levels, are seen as mere palliatives that may, in the medium term, only worsen matters while blinding us to inevitable doom; well-meaning attempts to ameliorate present poverty will only cause a more catastrophic loss of lives in the long term. "*Laissez-faire* is then the only ethically responsible approach to the problems of famine and hunger".[14]

Garret Hardin, one of the best-known neo-Malthusians, states:

> If poor countries received no food aid from outside, the rate of their growth would be periodically checked by crop failures and famines. But if they can always draw on a world food bank in time of need, their population can continue to grow unchecked, and so will their need for aid. In the short run a world food bank may diminish their need, but in the long run it actually increases that need without limit.[15]

Another argument which contradicts the very idea of finding reasons to combat extreme poverty bears a resemblance to the procedure known as "triage", a term by medical officers on the battlefront. Where there is a scarcity of doctors and a superabundance of

---

[14] O'Neill, *Faces of Hunger*, p. 17.
[15] Cited in O'Neill, op. cit., p. 58.

wounded, these are grouped into three categories: those who will probably survive without medical aid; those who might survive if they received it; and lastly, those who with the best possible medical attention are likely to die anyway. Only those who fall into the second category will receive medical assistance. The idea underlying the policy of triage is to use resources in the most efficient way possible. Those in the first category would surely survive without help, and since it is most unlikely that those in the third category would benefit from the resources, it would be wasteful to apply them.[16]

There has been the tendency to apply this idea to policies for combating poverty. It is not efficient to aid those sectors of society which have the means to get ahead without the help of a social policy; neither should we implement policies aimed at those in a situation of extreme poverty, since the most likely outcome is that the resources used in this manner will not be sufficient to rescue them from their plight. The ideal receivers are those at a fair distance above the absolute poverty line, who, like the wounded with slight injuries, are likely, with help, to substantially improve their situation.

There are several arguments for countering such neo-Malthusian opinions. The first refers to the alleged scarcity of food resources. Sen, for example, has recently shown that "in many large famines in the recent past, in which millions of people have died, there was no over-all decline in the amount of food availability at all, and the famines occurred precisely because of shifts in entitlements resulting from exercises of rights that are perfectly legitimate. [...] for many people the only resource that they legitimately possess, viz. their labor-power, may well turn out to be unsaleable in the market, giving the persons no command over food".[17] On the other hand, evidence that the birth rate is increasing in poor countries is also far from conclusive; rather, the trend would appear to be towards a fall, as has happened in the developed countries.[18]

TWO CONCEPTS OF POVERTY

While a variety of opinions exists regarding the perverse effects aid to poverty may entail, in 1971, a work was published which was to

---

[16] See P. Singer, *Practical Ethics*, p. 235
[17] A. Sen, "Rights and Capabilities", p. 134.
[18] See O. O'Neill, op. cit., p. 59.

throw fresh light on the question of distributive justice: this was John Rawls's *A Theory of Justice*. Thanks to Rawls, subjects such as the need for justice in the distribution of goods and services, for criteria of distribution, and the ideal of moving towards a more ordered and less unequal society permeated discussions on political and economic philosophy and ethics. The Harvard philosopher taught us that a just society is not only convenient, but rational. It is impossible to write about matters such as criteria of distribution, equality, rights and obligations of the State towards the "least advantaged" without reference to the work of Rawls. The present book is no exception. In order to explain and distinguish the concepts of poverty—both economically and ethically—we shall refer to two basic Rawlsean notions: the concept of "the least favored members of society", and that of "primary goods". Of the series of primary goods which this author classifies under five headings (the basic liberties, freedom of movement and of occupation, the powers and prerogatives of offices and positions of responsibility, income and wealth, and the social bases of self-respect), we shall be referring in particular to the last two, that is "income and wealth" and "the social bases of self-respect". While income and wealth allow us to examine the concept of poverty from an economic point of view, the social bases of self-respect draw us to its ethical dimension. Let us remember that, according to Rawls—and as we shall examine in greater depth in the next chapter—"primary goods are social background conditions and all-purpose means generally necessary for forming and rationally pursuing a conception of the good".[19] They are also defined as those things that "it is supposed a rational man wants whatever else he wants", since "regardless of what an individual's rational plans are in detail, it is assumed that there are various things which he would prefer more of rather than less".[20]

The Rawlsean conception of justice sets out from the idea that in order to found a well ordered society, individuals—finding themselves in a situation devoid of any privileged knowledge (Rawls describes them as behind a "veil of ignorance")—would, if they were rational, choose the following principles of justice:

---

[19] J. Rawls, "Social Unity and Primary Goods", pp. 362, 370.
[20] J. Rawls, *A Theory of Justice*, Cambridge: Harvard University Press, 1971, p. 92.

1. Each person has an equal right to the most extensive scheme of equal basic liberties compatible with a similar scheme of liberties for all.
2. Social and economic inequalities are to satisfy two conditions: they must be (a) to the greatest benefit of the least advantaged members of society; and (b) attached to offices and positions open to all under conditions of fair equality of opportunity.[21]

I shall leave for a later chapter certain reservations regarding Rawls's notion of primary goods and the plausibility of this notion as the basis for a theory of justice. Primary goods will here simply be taken as a reference point for developing the two concepts of poverty which I am interested in emphasizing.

Leaving the first principle—that of respect for the basic liberties—in the background, let us concentrate on the first part of the second principle in order to establish who are the least favored members of society. Now, to find out who the people in a state of extreme poverty (or in general in a state of poverty) are is no straightforward matter, and with the passing of the years has altered considerably.

POVERTY FROM THE ECONOMIC POINT OF VIEW

A good basis for a definition of poverty is that set forth by the European Commission in the first *Community Action Programme to Combat Poverty*. The definition is as follows: "The poor shall be taken to mean persons, families and groups of persons whose resources (material, cultural and social) are so limited as to exclude them from the minimum acceptable way of life in the Member States in which they live."[22]

Throughout this chapter we shall see that a number of criteria exist for defining what is "minimally acceptable". It will therefore be necessary to distinguish between different concepts related with poverty, such as, for example, moderate and extreme poverty, absolute and relative poverty.

a) Moderate and extreme poverty

Going back to Rawls, if we wish to identify the least advantaged individuals in a society we shall need to distinguish between moderate and extreme poverty, since individuals situated in the latter are

---

[21] J. Rawls, "Social Unity and Primary Goods", p. 362.
[22] Cited by Atkinson, op. cit., p. 126.

those who must be benefited in accordance with the principles of justice. Thus, according to Félix Vélez,

> The extreme poor are those persons who have an inadequate level of nutrition, resulting in a deficient level of physical and mental performance, which in turn prevents them from participating in the labor market or in intellectual activities such as education. The condition of extreme poverty also practically rules out any social mobility; the extreme poor are born and die generally in the same situation. The moderate poor, on the other hand, are those who, due to the degree of development of a country at a particular moment in time are not able to cover what they would regard as their basic needs. They differ from the extreme poor in having the capacity, but not the opportunities, to participate in economic and intellectual activities [...] Inhabitants in extreme poverty require immediate measures in order to leave their marginalization behind and to reduce their weakness and their vulnerability to the average.[23]

It is not difficult to draw the conclusion that people who live in a situation of extreme poverty are the least advantaged members of the less advantaged class.

Before continuing with our analysis, it is necessary to consider the primary good that refers to income and well-being. Rawls defines it as follows: "Income and wealth, understood broadly as they must be, are all-purpose means (having an exchange value) for achieving directly or indirectly a wide range of ends, whatever they may be"[24]

The situation of extreme poverty can be detected by means of several indicators such as the composition of the household by sex and age, the presence of illiteracy, the economic activity and income of families, the presence of invalids or handicapped individuals, access to basic services, to goods and the ownership of land and animals. As for income, a family is considered to be in a situation of extreme poverty when its *per capita* income is insufficient to purchase the Normative Food Basket.[25] Another way of measuring the degree of extreme poverty is on the basis of malnutrition. In the words of a Mexican economist:

---

[23] Félix Vélez. "Introducción", p. 9.

[24] J. Rawls, "Social Unity and Primary Goods", p. 366.

[25] In Mexico, the Normative Food Basket has been valued, since December 1997, at $241.70 a month (Mexican pesos). If the expansion factor is added, in which costs not destined to food consumption are included, the value of the basket increases to $323.32.

We define the extreme poor specifically as individuals who—taking into account their age and sex—cannot acquire sufficient nutrients to maintain their health and performance capacity. The required level of food intake is established at 2,250 calories a day per adult and 35.1 grams of proteins a day.[26]

Malnutrition and the list of goods regarded as essential represent two ways of defining the state of extreme poverty. This inclusion of diverse elements in order to establish a poverty line is an improvement on measurements based exclusively on income and consumption. As we shall see below, there are various ways of measuring poverty; and results differ in accordance with the method we decide to use.

On the other hand, it is indispensable to distinguish, in cases of extreme poverty, between chronic and temporary cases; this distinction is important, above all in countries like Mexico which possess an agriculture dependent on changing climatic factors. Temporary poverty is due, among other things, to economic crises due, for example, to a fall in prices or to natural phenomena such as droughts and floods. The distinction is important since the policies required to combat such cases may well be very different.

According to Santiago Levy, the situations of people undergoing extreme poverty can be distinguished in terms of seven characteristics:

1. The homes of extremely poor people have a higher fertility rate and a greater number of children.
2. People subject to extreme poverty cannot respond to a temporary fall in income. It is not possible for them to work more than already do; they thus have no means of compensating for times of economic depression.
3. Families in a situation of extreme poverty have a higher participation rate, applying to members of all ages, than the norm. The children of extremely poor families participate in economic activities from an early age. For them the cost of education is thus too high for them to meet.
4. The extremely poor have a lower capacity for dealing with risks and are subject to nutritional threats induced by a fall in income. Having little access to credit (as we shall see later on) and few tradable assets, any reduction in income results in an immediate drop in consumption.
5. The diet of extremely poor people is subject to alterations in line with its high degree of price and income elasticity of demand.
6. With regard to both adults and children, in extremely poor homes the level of nutrition has a direct effect on productivity.

---

[26] Santiago Levy, "La pobreza en México", p. 23.

7. Finally, the degree of inequality within families is greater in homes undergoing extreme poverty, since this situation determines how the additional resources for the family as a whole become allocated as resources for the various family members.[27]

b) Dysfunctional aspect of poverty

According to Debraj Ray,[28] the dysfunctional effect of poverty on the economy at large is what interests most countries in fighting it; poverty—so it is claimed—constitutes a brake on a country's economic development. This dysfunctional aspect is reflected principally in three factors affecting the poor: their possibilities of obtaining credit, the sale of their labor power, and the rent of land for food production.

The credit market is practically nonexistent in those places where people live in a situation of extreme poverty; this is due to two reasons. The first consists in the fact that the poor lack the necessary guarantees for obtaining loans. The word "guarantee" can be understood in two ways. On the one hand it presupposes the existence of a project for which credit is needed; however, if this does not produce successful results, the borrower will lack the resources to pay back the loan. On the other hand, poor people lack the means for obtaining insurance to indemnify them against the failure of the project. This lack of a guarantee, in both senses, prevents people from requesting loans and credit from being granted.[29] The second reason is that in the case of poor people the incentive to pay the debt is extremely limited since each additional unit of money means much more to them than to the lender; this causes a reduction in marginal utility. The scant access to credit also affects the access of poor people to land markets.

On the other hand, the sale of labor power, as we shall see below, is intimately connected to the problem of malnutrition.

Finally, the problem of the rent of the land contains in itself all the obstacles detected for the award of credit. If the poor lack the capacity to face up to the threat of failure of an economic project, the incentives to rent land are considerably reduced. On the other hand,

---

[27] Santiago Levy, "La pobreza extrema en México: una propuesta de política", pp. 69–73.

[28] See D. Ray, *Development Economics*, p. 267.

[29] Ibid., pp. 267–270.

peasants have extremely restricted options. If they own their own land they will generally produce for self consumption; if they do not they will have to sell their labor which, in cases of extreme poverty will be of reduced value as a result of malnutrition.

c) Absolute and relative poverty

A widely discussed matter in studies of poverty is whether this should be conceived in absolute and relative terms. Of course there is always an absolute element in the notion of poverty. People, irrespective of the society in which they live, need to obtain adequate levels of food, clothing and housing. We cannot deny the existence of a biological imperative to satisfy needs such as nutrition and health; nevertheless, it is possible to accept that variations might exist regarding what is considered "adequate" in different societies. In some cases, such variations respond to the specific characteristics of each society being studied; in others to the actual prevailing socioeconomic conditions. Given such differences between countries, it is not surprising that a variety of yardsticks exists; we see the need to draw poverty lines sharing common properties but which might vary from one country to another.[30]

Robert MacNamara, as president of the World Bank, stressed the importance of distinguishing between absolute and relative poverty. The latter is something that exists in industrialized countries, in the sense that some citizens are poorer than their neighbors. Likewise, people who live in a state of relative poverty in Australia may be better off than pensioners living in Great Britain, while these are not poor if we compare them with poor people in African countries. As Peter Singer explains "Absolute poverty [...] is poverty by any standard". He goes on to quote MacNamara:

> Poverty at the absolute level [...] is life at the very margin of existence. The absolute poor are severely deprived human beings struggling to survive in a set of squalid and degraded circumstances almost beyond the power of our sophisticated imaginations and privileged circumstances to conceive. Compared to those fortunate enough to live in developed countries, individuals in the poorest nations have: An infant mortality rate eight times higher; A life expectancy one-third lower; An adult illiteracy rate 60 per cent less; A nutritional level, for one out of every two in the population, below acceptable standards; And for millions of in-

---

[30] See D. Ray, op. cit., p. 250–251.

fants, less protein than is sufficient to permit optimum development of the brain.[31]

This is no trivial matter. Amartya Sen has shown us some attempts at measuring poverty by means of the average fall or rise in real wages.[32] Others have regarded poverty in relative terms because they confuse it with inequality, and thus see it as a misfortune impossible to eliminate. Thus when the poverty line is set in accordance with the average income, there will always be poor people, "relatively speaking". Furthermore, some thinkers have sought a psychological explanation in order to argue in favor of the "relativity" of poverty. Sen demonstrates this with the following statement by Dr. Rhodes Boyson, British Social Security Minister under Margaret Thatcher:

> Those on the poverty line in the United States earn more than 50 times the average income of someone in India. This is what relative poverty is all about […]. Apparently, the more people earn, the more they believe poverty exists, presumably so they can be pleased about the fact that it is not themselves who are poor.[33]

Poverty lines usually include, as we shall see below, notions regarding what is necessary or what constitutes a basic need. Such notions need to be studied with great care, since upon them will depend what is finally incorporated as necessary for functioning in life. Two traditional ways of measuring poverty are the "head-count ratio", which assesses the proportion of the population which is below the poverty line, and the "income-gap ratio", which measures "the average income shortfall of all the poor taken together as a proportion of the poverty line itself, or alternatively as a proportion of the mean income of the community".[34] Nonetheless, all such measures confuse poverty with inequality and could lead to absurd results: let us suppose all incomes in a particular country were to fall in the same proportion, leaving half the population in a famine situation; an assessment of poverty based on equality would simply register it as stable. According to Sen:

---

[31] Cited in P. Singer, *Practical Ethics*, pp. 218–219.

[32] See Amartya Sen, *The Standard of Living*, p. 17.

[33] Ibid., p. 18.

[34] Amartya Sen, "Poor, Relatively Speaking", p. 340.

...there is an irreducible core of *absolute* deprivation in our idea of poverty , which translates reports of starvation, malnutrition and visible hardship into a diagnosis of poverty without having to ascertain first the relative picture. Thus the approach of relative deprivation supplements rather than supplants the analysis of poverty in terms of absolute dispossession.[35]

Recently, Sen has continued arguing for the existence of an absolute nucleus in the idea of poverty:

If there is starvation and hunger, then—no matter what the *relative* picture looks like, there clearly is poverty. [...] Even when we shift our attention from hunger and look at other aspects of living standard, the absolutist aspect of poverty does not disappear.[36]

E. Hernández Laos, referring to this passage, comments: "thus, in the adequate approach to the analysis of poverty, what must be considered is neither the satisfiers not their utility but what Sen calls the *capabilities* of people to *function* in society; that is, their abilities to do things using means and resources to do so". [37] As we shall see further on, the concepts of capabilities and functionings constitute the nucleus of Sen's theory.

Another important element for measuring poverty consists in establishing a unit of measurement, which, in the case we are considering, may be households or individuals. It often happens that the only indicators we have for establishing a poverty line are income and consumption. In this way the consumption of households is expressed in terms of the average consumption for each member of the family. This way of measuring consumption overlooks a very important aspect: that the distribution of expenditures within the household is often distorted. A serious study of poverty ought to measure the inequality existing within households, which is frequently to the detriment of women and old people. Likewise, within consumption, scales of equivalence by age ought to be established.

We can conclude that the notion of absolute poverty is indispensable for planning social programs, especially in countries facing severe failure to satisfy basic needs, irrespective of cultural or social differences. The following will show that absolute poverty is inti-

---

[35] A. Sen, *Poverty and Famines. An Essay on Entitlement and Deprivation*, p. 17.

[36] A. Sen, "Poor, Relatively Speaking", pp. 332–333.

[37] E. Hernández Laos, "Retos para la medición de la pobreza en México".

mately related to two factors that set it in a vicious circle: malnutrition and the rising birth rate.

d) Vicious circles of poverty

It is impossible to approach the subject of poverty without mentioning two phenomena that lead to a vicious circle: malnutrition and the increase in the birth rate.

A close relation exists between poverty and malnutrition, especially in countries where a large number of people are living below the extreme poverty line. When individuals lack the indispensable income for satisfying their basic needs it is difficult for them to acquire adequate levels of food. However, as Debraj Ray[38] affirms, the concept of an "acceptable level" is not a completely neutral one, since it depends on the class of activity people are engaged in, and on their nutritional background. Even in cases where it is believed that an "acceptable level" exists, it is possible to find indicators of malnutrition, particularly in children. Now, it is important to bear in mind that the relation between malnutrition and income is not always direct. An increase in income does not necessarily imply a decrease in malnutrition. It is thus necessary for malnutrition to be attacked directly via food supplements.

The phenomenon of malnutrition may produce two effects. The first has to do with the value good nutrition has in itself; to be well-fed is desirable because it fosters good mental and physical health and better resistance to disease. Nutrition is also connected with the utility it provides, principally in the functional sense; good food raises the capacity for work, and thus the possibility of obtaining income.

The second effect involves the preferences that individuals manifest for certain types of food, whether because of superior flavor, effective marketing, or because being in a position to consume them imparts social and economic prestige. It is thus necessary to approach the problem of the causes of malnutrition taking into account the two above-mentioned effects. On the one hand, it is necessary to demonstrate the need to consume foods that provide the amount of calories and proteins necessary for the organism to function well; on the other, it is important to plan educational policies on food; thus

---

[38] D. Ray, op. cit., p. 250.

helping people to distinguish between those which help to combat malnutrition and those promoted by advertising campaigns and which derive much of their selling power from the idea that they improve one's social image. As we shall see further on and as Len Doyal points out:

People do have strong feelings about what they need, and these feelings can vary enormously between cultures. Conflicting evidence of this kind suggests that subjective feeling is not a reliable determination of human need, a point reinforced by the fact that we can strongly desire things that are seriously harmful and, in our ignorance, not desire things that we require to avoid such harm.[39]

Thus knowledge regarding the consumption of food that provides the calories and proteins necessary for the body to function adequately is a matter for education. The effects of malnutrition are variable, including, for example, retardation of growth and muscular development, tendency to fall ill, vulnerability to infections and reduction of the capacity for work. Undernourished people get tired easily, suffer brusque changes of character manifested as mental apathy, depression, introversion and reduced intellectual capacity and lack of motivation. A condition intimately related to malnutrition is lack of energy.

The importance of the biological relation between nutrition and the capacity to work is due to the fact that inadequate nutrition increases the likelihood of obtaining low wages, and low wages lead to greater malnutrition. This is where the dysfunctional aspect of malnutrition lies. Regardless of whether the problem of adequate nutrition is of a social and ethical nature, in itself it has an impact on the possibility of obtaining income.[40]

Another vicious circle of poverty lies in its relation with the rising birth rate. In practically all countries where extreme poverty is found, it has been detected that households contain large numbers of people, among whom the majority are children. Clearly the size of the family can be the cause of poverty, but it may also be one of its effects. The largest families, especially those with most children, have a lower per capita income level. One of the ways in which such families try to improve their incomes is through putting their chil-

---

[39] Len Doyal "A Theory of Human Need", p. 157.
[40] See D. Ray, op. cit., p. 275.

dren to work, but this has little effect on the per capita level, since child labor is so poorly paid. Childhood labor exemplifies the vicious circle which links poverty with a rising birth rate, since it is common for families to have a large number of children as a means of increasing their income; yet, since the additional income is at such a low rate, the *per capita* level falls. There has, however, been some criticism of the relation drawn between poverty and family size. Debraj Ray, for instance, criticizes the use of the notion of *per capita* expenditure (or income) as the relevant indicator of the poverty line; since children also consume less, this averaging out of family income and expenditure tends to overstate the degree of poverty. Ray also points out that we should make allowances for the significant economies of scale enjoyed by large families; the failure to do so, once again, leads to an exaggeration of the degree of poverty. It is important for studies of poverty to take into consideration such economies of scale, and to try to measure them. One way of doing so "is to try different parametric values for returns to scale and see if 'reasonable' values overturn the observed correlation between poverty and household size". Ray also notes that women tend to be over-represented as heads of poor families.[41]

In spite of these two criticisms, the relation existing between poverty and the birth rate has been studied by economists. This is what Levy tells us:

> In poor homes, children mean future security for their parents and, after five or six years, an additional source of labor. There is increasing evidence that high fertility is a consequence of characteristics associated with poverty, particularly a high rate of infant mortality. Having more children [...] *can be interpreted as a response by parents to the high rate of infant mortality.*[42]

In fact there are two kinds of motivation to reproduce, above all in poor countries. The first regards children as such; in other words, it maintains that it is "essential" for a couple to have children, that these are an object of satisfaction and joy in themselves. This idea may also be supported by the religious thesis that people ought to be ready to have all the children that God sends them. The second motivation is that children represent a sort of insurance for old age. Chil-

---

[41] D. Ray, op. cit., pp. 258–259.
[42] S. Levy, "La pobreza extrema en México: una propuesta política", p. 70.

dren may indeed offer the assurance of economic support in regions where social security is non-existent. It tends to be the case that, where this mentality exists, the preference for male children over females leads to discriminatory behavior.

Another important factor tending to raise the rate of family increase is that, as we have already noted, children may be seen as producers of wealth. Children born to impoverished families, especially in hostile geographic environments, often start to work as young as six years old. Their tasks may include, for example, looking after smaller brothers and sisters, tending to domestic animals, fetching water and collecting firewood: in other words, participating in the activities necessary for the family's survival.[43]

In order to escape from the vicious circle of poverty it is essential to pay attention to two aspects: implementing food campaigns which clearly indicate which are the items that contribute to eliminating malnutrition; and strengthening general education, since this is intimately related to the birth rate. The value of education is one of the ideas brandished against neo-Malthusian theses.

e) Measurement of poverty

One of the most important aspects of the study of poverty is the methodology of detection. Two methods in particular have been used to measure poverty. Dasgupta has explained that "the most common practice in measuring the extent of poverty in a community or society is to select a cut-off level of income below which a person or household is deemed to be poor (the *poverty level*) and to estimate the percentage of the population whose income is below it. This is the *headcount index*".[44] Another method consists in establishing a *poverty gap*. The idea underlying this is "to sum over each poor person the gap between the poverty level and her income, and then express the sum as a percentage of the total income [...] of the population. [...] The poverty gap is the minimum amount of additional income expressed as a percentage of society's aggregate income, which, if it is obtained by the poor, can eliminate poverty".[45] Dasgupta, however, proposes a series of indicators which would allow us

---

[43] See P. Dasgupta, *An Inquiry into Well-Being and Destitution*, pp. 356–359.
[44] Ibid., p. 78.
[45] Ibid., pp. 78–79.

to go beyond the analysis characteristic of most economics-based studies of poverty. The first indicator is provided by aggregating nutrition, housing, clothing, drinking water, medical care and, in general, environmental resources; these are what is needed for survival. The second indicator is made up of indices which aim to measure the political and civil liberties enjoyed by the members of a society. This indicator consists in studying the degree to which individuals can play an active and critical role in the selection of economic, political and legal structures; to what degree they are protected against arbitrary arrest, physical injury by others and afforded the protection of their legally acquired property. Finally, the third indicator consists of what Dasgupta refers to as *achievements*. Such achievements include high rates of literacy, infant survival, life expectancy. They also include reduction of discrimination and internal conflicts.[46]

One of the most widely accepted criteria for measuring living conditions is based on expenditure and consumption. As Skoufias, Davis and Behrman mention:

> The main theoretical reasoning behind this argument is that, in accordance with the theory of consumption, it is more likely that estimates based on current consumption provide a more reliable basis for estimation of the household's permanent income (sustainable standard of living) than estimates based on current income [...] Consumption measures that which people receive, and so if one is interested in measuring individuals' living conditions, this may be a better yardstick than income. For these reasons, consumption indicators are used [...] as the means of measuring household well-being.[47]

Likewise, consumption shows the preferences of individuals, and is thus easier to observe. It seems reasonable to state that if the members of a community prefer certain goods and services this is because such goods and services increase their utility. Besides, other criteria exist for measuring poverty which aim to take into account, on the one hand, a more complete vision of the human being, and on the other, the context in which they find themselves, accepting that in cases of measurement of poverty normative aspects also come into play.

---

[46] Cf. ibid., p. 38.
[47] E. Skoufias, B. Davis and J. Behrman, "Evaluación del sistema de selección de familias beneficiarias de PROGRESA", p. 83.

In Mexico, one of the researchers who has worked most in the discussion of methods for measuring poverty is Julio Boltvinik.[48] Naturally, the present study refers only to a few of the methods studied by this author, and in a fairly summary fashion. It is important to note that a great variety of approaches exists to the problem of detecting and fighting poverty in different countries; a complete study would go far beyond the limits of the present book.[49]

As we have already mentioned, one of the most widely used methods is that of the Poverty Line, which establishes a Normative Food Basket, calculates its cost and multiplies it by the proportion of income or expenditure devoted to foodstuffs. A variant of the same method exists, which involves a Normative Basket including a larger number of goods. This variant has been called the Normative Basket of Essential Satisfiers or Generalized Normative Basket. The problem noted by Boltvinik is that when these variants are applied, only food poverty is being assessed and other aspects of poverty are ignored.[50] He also considers a variant of the Generalized Normative Basket which consists in determining the list of goods and services required by a household of a certain size and in a certain time. The problem presented by these bases for measurements is that the list of goods and services they include may suffer modifications so that the poverty line established by them may cease to be a true reflection of what families require.

Apart from poverty lines, Boltvinik considers some variants of the Multidimensional Models of Unsatisfied Basic Needs. He calls the first the Original Restricted Variant. As its name suggests, the range and variety of indicators is rather narrow. By means of this variant poor families are identified on the basis of a generally absolute concept of poverty. Thus each indicator is of a binary nature, offering only two options: above the threshold (which can be represented by a score of 0) and below the threshold (with a score of 1); poor house-

---

[48] See J. Boltvinik. "Métodos de medición de la pobreza. Conceptos y tipología"; "Métodos de medición de la pobreza. Una evaluación crítica"; and "Opciones metodológicas para medir la pobreza en México", pp. 869–878. These methods use a formulation in economic terms which exceeds the scope of the present work.

[49] For the complete schematic details of the different ways of measuring poverty, see J. Boltvinik. "Métodos de medición de la pobreza. Conceptos y tipología".

[50] J. Boltvinik. "Métodos de medición de la pobreza. Una evaluación crítica", p. 86.

holds are those with at least one indicator below the threshold.[51] The variant of this method presents a number of problems, foremost among which is the supposition that basic needs comprise only certain, generally very limited, sources of household well-being. This gives us a partial and not an overall view of poverty.

There is also the Improved Restricted Variant of Basic Needs. Among other things, this enables the poverty gap to be calculated; it operates with a larger number of indicators of shortfalls and introduces a procedure of expectations in order to decide the levels of the thresholds beneath which the poor are to be found. Thus the thresholds of a particular item will vary according to the levels attained in a particular society.[52]

On the other hand, the Original General Variant of Unsatisfied Basic Needs sets out to verify directly the satisfaction of all human needs. Three groups of poor people are identified on the basis of the studies carried out: those who are poor according to the criteria of both the Unsatisfied Basic Needs and the Basic Basket; and those who are poor under the criteria of either one or the other method. Boltvinik considers, however, that this variant suffers from the same defects as the two previously mentioned methods.

Finally, Boltvinik proposes the Integrated Method for Measuring poverty. The application of this method enables a broader concept of poverty to be defined as a result of combining the Improved Restricted Variant of Unsatisfied Basic Needs with the Generalized Normative Basket and the Modified Poverty Line in order to achieve an indicator which reflects both what people are objectively seen to need and their own perception of their needs. The method also takes into consideration, for example, excessive working hours, thus enabling us to obtain an integrated household poverty index, and likewise to calculate all the yardsticks of poverty, their incidence of occurrence, and the dimensions of the gap separating the poor and the non-poor. The index may also be broken down, thus enabling the contribution of each dimension of privation to be calculated.[53]

---

[51] See J. Boltvinik, "Métodos de medición de la pobreza: Conceptos y tipología", p. 48.
[52] Ibid., p. 49.
[53] Ibid., p. 55

As we may observe, these criteria for measuring poverty embrace a series of indicators which go a long way beyond income and consumption. This leads us to the consideration that any line we establish between those who are really poor and those who are not will depend upon the definition of poverty we adopt and the means we employ to measure it. It is important to stress, too, that the adoption of one way of measuring poverty rather than another responds to sectoral interests. While methods for measuring poverty help us to implement public policies to combat it, we should not forget that the "choice" of one method or another will have practical repercussions which may be undesirable. The methods help us to decide who are poor and who are not; an inadequate method may leave certain people who really need assistance without it.

Amartya Sen warns us of the danger of using merely quantitative methods when he states that positive economics has not managed to describe the facts objectively; its descriptions are always permeated by value judgments. In Sen's own words:

> Description isn't just observing and reporting; it involves the exercise—possibly difficult—of selection. For example, in judging F.M. Eden's 1797 study *The State of the Poor*, or Friedrich Engels' *The Condition of the working Class in England in 1844*, or John and Barbara Hammonds' *The Village Labourer 1760–1832*, a good deal more is involved than just checking the truth of the individual facts recorded.[54]

It must be pointed out that positions such as that of Dasgupta take into consideration characteristics of human beings that must be attended to and which go beyond merely economic aspects and those of survival: for example, political and civil liberties. As the first of Rawls's principles of justice states, it is not possible to attain a less unequal society without respect for basic liberties.

We shall now pass on to consider the evaluative character which underlies the mechanisms used for identifying the "extreme poor", and to analyze the primary good which has to do with the social bases of self-respect.

---

[54] A. Sen, "Description as Choice", p. 433.

POVERTY FROM THE ETHICAL POINT OF VIEW

As we have already observed, the primary goods that enter into play in discussions of poverty include some which are of a moral rather than an economic nature. In this connection Rawls notes:

> The social bases of self-respect are those aspects of basic institutions that are normally essential if citizens are to have a lively sense of their own worth as moral persons and to be able to realize their highest-order interests and advance their ends with self-confidence.[55]

Elsewhere he affirms:

> We may define self-respect (or self-esteem) as having two aspects. First of all [...] it includes a person's sense of his own value, his secure conviction that his conception of his good, his plan of life, is worth carrying out. And second, self-respect implies a confidence in one's ability, so far as it is in one's power, to fulfill one's intentions. When we feel that our plans are of little value, we cannot pursue them with pleasure or take delight in their execution. Nor plagued by failure and self-doubt can we continue in our endeavors.[56]

It is worth noting that, as we shall examine more thoroughly in the following chapters, philosophers who concern themselves with matters involving distributive justice have emphasized the ethical aspect of poverty. Amartya Sen has insisted that the purposes of any theory of justice must include the development of capacities, which are what enable human beings not only to do but to be—in other terms, to exercise both negative and positive liberty, thus becoming participative agents in social life. Martha Nussbaum has expressed the need to distribute the goods and services that are indispensable for people to cover their essential basic needs and thus enable them to realize their potential as human beings. Ronald Dworkin has proposed that any distribution must take into account the integrity of individuals, including their physical safety, the maintenance of the body and the preservation of health; it must also respect that integrity of persons which is involved in the exercise of preferences—in other words, when possibilities for choice are widened—and, likewise, the integrity of people's self-image. Len Doyal has stressed the value of the autonomy of men and women as a basic need, enabling them, among

---

[55] J. Rawls, "Social Unity and Primary Goods", p. 366.
[56] J. Rawls, *A Theory of Justice*, p. 92.

other matters, to have sufficient self-confidence to *want* to act and participate in the society or culture to which they belong. Onora O'Neill has insisted on the fact that poverty places people in a situation of vulnerability which prevents them from being able to refuse what is offered them by those in power. In her opinion we find ourselves on the way to a just society when we achieve policies of war against poverty that can be refused because other options exist.

We can thus affirm that, while the economic approach is indispensable for studying poverty, we cannot leave the ethical aspect aside; in the opinion of the present writer, this is the most important thing of all, as it centers on individuals' autonomy and their possibilities for choice.

The concept of respect, in philosophy, has its origins in Kantian thought. Two ideas of Kant's allow us to approach the notion of the respect that all human beings deserve: the concept of autonomy and that of the treatment of people as ends, and not merely as means, which appears in the second formulation of the categorical imperative. As regards autonomy, Kant defined this as the property belonging to the will of being a law unto itself (regardless of all the properties of the objects of desire). Kant holds that autonomy, thus understood, is the supreme principle of morality, inasmuch as it is the necessary condition for a categorical imperative. He tells us: "Autonomy of the will is the property the will has of being a law unto itself (independently of every property belonging to the objects of volition). Hence the principle of autonomy is 'Never to choose except in such a way that in the same volition the maxims of your choice are also present as universal law'".[57]

Part of Kant's work on morality aims at demonstrating the legitimacy of attributing autonomy to the will of all rational agents, human will being included. Autonomy is the capacity of rational agents to establish laws they themselves obey. In this sense it is the necessary condition for liberty.

In relation with the idea of the treatment of persons as ends, Kant tells us in the *Groundwork of the Metaphysic of Morals*:

> [M]an, and in general every rational being, *exists* as an end in himself, *not merely as a means* for arbitrary use by this or that will: he must in all his actions, whether they are directed to himself or to other rational beings, always be viewed

---

[57] Immanuel Kant, *Groundwork of the Metaphysic of Morals*, p. 108.

at the same time as an end [...] Rational beings [...], are called *persons* because their nature already marks them out as ends in themselves—that is as something that ought not too be used merely as a means—and consequently imposes to that extent a limit on all arbitrary treatment of them (and is an object of reverence). Person, therefore, are not merely subjective ends whose existence as an object of our actions has a value *for us*. They are *objective ends*—that is, things whose existence is itself an end, and indeed an end such that in its place we can put no other end to which they should serve *simply* as means; for unless this is so, nothing at all of *absolute* value would be found anywhere. But if all value were conditioned—that is contingent—then no supreme principle could be found for reason at all.[58]

For Kant, rational nature is an end in itself and there are no valid arguments for treating it exclusively as a means for other rational beings to achieve their ends. Further on, Kant tells us that the practical imperative must be as follows: "Act in such a way that you always treat humanity, whether in your own person or in the person of any other, never simply as a means, but always at the same time as an end".[59]

According to Kant the concept of the rational being who must be considered a universal legislator and who can judge himself and sit in judgment on his acts, leads to the concept of the "kingdom of ends". The kingdom of ends is "a systematic union of different rational beings under common laws".[60]

Kant's idea of autonomy has been set in opposition to certain conceptions of utilitarianism which enable us, on certain occasions, to ignore the ends of people if we can thus obtain, for example, a social utility. A social gain compensates for the loss of utility that may be suffered by certain people. The Kantian thesis commits us to respect each and every person, irrespective of social utility. Rawls's first principle of justice, which is based on liberties, and Nozick's idea of moral constraints[61] show us the incompatibility of certain utilitarian principles with the idea of the respect which we owe to people because they must be treated as ends and not exclusively as means.

In Bernard Williams's words, "Kant's point of view not only carries to the limit the notion that moral worth cannot depend on con-

---

[58] Ibid., p. 95.
[59] Ibid., p. 96.
[60] Ibid., p. 100.
[61] See Robert Nozick, *Anarchy, State and Utopia*, pp. 28–33.

tingencies, but also emphasizes, in its picture of the Kingdom of Ends, the idea of *respect* which is owed to each man as a rational moral agent—and, since men are equally such agents, is owed equally to all…".[62]

One philosopher who has dealt with the subject of respect is Avishai Margalit,[63] who seeks to clarify precisely what aspect of human beings it is which justifies their deserving respect simply on account of being human. He examines three classes of justifications which have been offered regarding the respect due to persons: the positive, skeptical and negative justifications.

The positive justification is based in part on the notion of "reflected glory"; this has two components: the first is of a religious nature and affirms that human beings have been created in the image of God and thus deserve to be respected. The defenders of this idea say that it is not man as such who deserves respect, but rather the degree to which mankind is a "reflection of God". The second component refers to the "achievements of man", and is based on the belief that humanity has achieved great attainments in all fields, and that the glory of these achievements touches all those who belong to the human species. "If Buddha, Aristotle, Mozart, Shakespeare, and Newton constitute peaks of humanity, we participate in their glory even if we are only on the slopes."[64]

Margalit tells us that "Any trait that is a candidate for justifying the requirement of treating all human beings with respect must satisfy the following constraints:

1. It "must not be graded, since respect must be given equally to all human beings", i.e. there cannot be people of first and second class according to race, religious beliefs, gender or sexual preferences.
2. It "must not be of the sort that can be abused—namely, that can provide a reason for abhorrence or disrespect". In other words, it cannot be based on the idea that any human being, by the very fact of being such, may carry out actions regarded as not moral without any justification.
3. It "must be morally relevant to respecting humans"; i.e. it must incorporate those aspects which justify respect on moral grounds.

---

[62] See B. Williams, "The Idea of Equality", p. 235.
[63] A. Margalit, *The Decent Society*.
[64] Ibid., p. 59.

4.   It "must provide a humanistic justification for respect—that is, the justification must be made only in human terms, without appealing to divine entities".[65]

As we have already seen, another element of positive justification is found in the ethics of Kant. Margalit, too, refers to Kant's specification of the components that give value to humanity: 1) "being a creature who determines ends, that is, a creature who gives things value; 2) "being a creature with the capacity for self-legislation"; 3) "having the ability to perfect oneself—that is, to achieve greater and greater perfection"; 4) "having the capacity to be a moral agent"; 5) "being rational"; 6) "being the only creature capable of transcending natural causality".[66]

To these characteristics we could add, with Bernard Williams, that the humanity of human beings lies in their being "necessarily to some extent conscious of themselves and of the world they live in"; though, as Williams also points out, this should not be taken to mean that all "men are equally conscious of themselves and of their situation". The importance of Williams's idea is that the social condition and the environment exercise a direct influence on the consciousness that people have of themselves and of the environment in which they live.[67] The inclusion of the situation of the person, of his or her social condition and environment is of the greatest importance for the study of poverty. For example, certain geographical conditions prevent people from being really capable of transcending natural causality. Scarcity of water is a good example.

The skeptical solution, on the other hand, is based on the fact that in our form of life individuals believe that human beings deserve respect. According to this point of view, human beings are valuable "because others value them, and not because of any prior characteristic that justifies such valuing".[68] A complementary aspect of this justification lies in considering respect for "all" persons irrespective of the social group to which they belong.

Finally, the negative justification consists in rejecting the theses that set out to treat human beings as if they were not human. This justification is founded in the way in which we view human beings.

---

[65] Ibid., pp. 62–63.

[66] Ibid., p. 63.

[67] B. Williams, op. cit., pp. 237–238.

[68] A. Margalit, op. cit., p. 77.

When a society fails to see a person as a human being, it is a society which humiliates. This means having the attitudes of exploiters, of people who treat others as if they were machines, of people who stigmatize certain persons on the grounds certain diseases, the color of their skins, race, sexual orientations, etc. In Margalit's words, societies that treat certain sections of the population as if they were not human are those that humiliate:

The key concept for humiliation is rejection from the human commonwealth. But such rejection is not based on a belief or attitude that the rejected person is merely an object or an animal. The rejection consists [in] behaving *as if* the person were an object or an animal. Such rejection typically consists in treating human beings as subhuman.[69]

Now, there are certain conclusion that can be reached from the arguments set forth above. Perhaps the easiest position to reject is that of the "achievements of mankind". There are two reasons for doing so; the first is that talent is not equally distributed; the second is that in the same way as mankind produces "achievements" it also generates inhuman horrors. There is no reason why we should be proud of the compositions of Mozart and not feel ashamed of the crimes committed by the Nazis.

The "image of God" argument has enjoyed considerable acceptance. As was mentioned at the beginning of this chapter, one reason for combating poverty is based on certain religious beliefs. The problem with this argument is that, on the one hand, it does not take into consideration the intrinsic value of man, and on the other it cannot be accepted by individuals who lack such beliefs.

In this sense, Kant's idea seems to have a certain weight: we cannot treat other people merely as means, but as ends in themselves. The theses held by Margalit are also important; it is essential to see persons as persons with consciousness of themselves and their environment.

We can conclude that poverty diminishes the ability of persons to exercise their rationality, their will, to set themselves purposes and to seek the most adequate means to realize such purposes. In Margalit's words, a society that permits cases of extreme poverty to exist is a society that humiliates, it is thus not "decent".

---

[69] Ibid., p. 112.

Both policies to combat poverty and the means to implement them must act with respect for persons in mind. Any social policy that fails to take into account the moral dimension of poverty runs the risk of failure. The struggle against poverty must seek a means of improving individuals' income and well-being, but also of offering them the necessary means for developing their autonomy, of enabling them to establish their own life plans and seek adequate means to carry them out; finally such a struggle must seek to establish and to broaden the social bases of self-respect.

Now that we have examined an economic concept of poverty and an ethical one, we shall go on to outline one of the programs implemented in Mexico with the aim of combating extreme poverty.

PROGRESA: A PROGRAM DESIGNED TO COMBAT EXTREME POVERTY

The Mexican Government's Education, Health and Food Program,[70] to which I refer, was assigned the following characteristics:

- Its aim was to combat extreme poverty among families living in rural zones of Mexico. A number of indicators exist for identifying families that find themselves in a situation of extreme poverty and marginalization. One such indicator is the impossibility of earning sufficient *per capita* income to acquire the Normative Food Basket[71] which, since 1997, has been set at 323.32 pesos (less than 30 US dollars) a month; this figure includes both food costs and some non-food costs. Other indicators of poverty are the percentage of the population over 15 years which is illiterate; that of dwellings without piped water, drainage, or electricity; that of dwellings with earth floor; the average number of people sharing a room; and the proportion of members of households occupied in the primary sector, both by sex and by age. The program gives special attention to the presence of illiteracy and, above all, the individuals' access to health services.
- It was aimed at rural communities, defined as localities with less than 2,500 inhabitants; this was because the majority of households in extreme poverty are concentrated in the countryside.
- The program is implemented by a coordinating body (CONPROGRESA) in which the Public Education, Health, and Social Development Ministries all participated, as well as the IMSS-Solidaridad program (which brings together the Mexican Health and Social Security Institute and the "Solidarity program set

[70] PROGRESA (*Programa de Educación, Salud y Alimentación*) was set up in August, 1997, by decree of President Zedillo.
[71] The Bank of Mexico is responsible for establishing the value of the Basic Food Basket.

up under the previous president, Carlos Salinas de Gortari). The involvement of several public institutions was of great importance since the aim was to combat poverty in a comprehensive manner.

- The program has a gender approach; that is to say its program was focused on the women who look after homes. This aspect was innovatory and responded to the observation that within marginalized groups there are subgroups—women being one—that are even more marginalized. Likewise, the relationship between the Coordination and the communities is channeled via a community promoter elected by the members of the community itself.
- All communities must have education and health services, in other words, they must have at least one classroom for primary school and distance-learning facilities for secondary education [*telesecundaria*], as well as a dispensary, a small hospital or mobile clinic. This condition has been problematic since some populations situated in the most marginalized zones of the country remained beyond the Program's reach.
- The Program demands the co-responsibility of beneficiaries. This takes the form of a firm commitment by the latter to send their children to school, attend the talks on preventive medicine, not to miss medical appointments and to spend the monetary support strictly on improvements to family life.
- PROGRESA was designed with both long and short-term aims. The first consisted in providing support to help benefited household members rise above the conditions of extreme poverty. The second involved the promotion of education and health in the expectation that later on beneficiaries would have the possibility of abandoning their situation of marginalization and escaping from the vicious circles of poverty mentioned above.
- The program is focalized. This means that surveys were carried out throughout Mexico to identify households in a situation of extreme poverty. Since resources available for fighting poverty will, even in the best of cases, inevitably be limited, it is indispensable to ensure that beneficiaries are the people who most need them.[72]

Support is given for a period of three years with the possibility of extension by a further three years. At present 2 million Mexican families are beneficiaries of PROGRESA.

In order to harmonize actions in the fields of education, health and nutrition, the assistance provided by PROGRESA has three components:

- Educational support which enable children and young people to receive complete basic education, fostering their registration, regular attendance at school, and the participation of their parents in helping them get the most out of their schooling.

---

[72] See J. Gómez de Léon, D. Hernández and G. Vázquez. "El Programa de Educación, Salud y Alimentación: orientaciones y componentes", p. 12.

- Attention to the health of all family members, while promoting a new attitude to the use of the health services, generating a predominantly preventive approach.
- Support for improvement of eating habits and the nutritional state of the members of the families with least resources.

It is important to point out that PROGRESA, following a distinction made by Jon Elster, aims to form part of a schema of global justice. This Norwegian philosopher distinguishes between global and local justice:

> globally redistributive policies are characterized by three features. First, they are designed centrally, at the level of the national government. Second, they are intended to compensate people for various sorts of bad luck, resulting from the possession of 'morally arbitrary properties'. Third, they typically take the form of cash transfers. Principles of local justice [on the other hand] are designed by relatively autonomous institutions which, although they may be constrained by guidelines laid down by the center, have some autonomy to design and implement their preferred scheme. Also, they are not compensatory, or only partially so. A scheme for allocating scarce medical resources may compensate patients for bad medical luck, but not for other kinds of bad luck [...]. Finally, local justice concerns allocations in kind of goods (and burdens), not of money.[73]

Since PROGRESA is a national program, aimed at families living in situations of extreme poverty and marginalization, and providing monetary transferences, it falls unquestionably into the category of global justice.

At this point we would do well to examine some of the problems that occur in the application of PROGRESA. First of all, there is a degree of ambiguity in the way of measuring poverty. While needs, capacities, preferences are taken into account, the yardstick used—as the evaluation document makes clear—was consumption. As Skoufias, B. Davis and J. Berhrman state:

> As economists we tend to emphasize measurements of poverty based on consumption [...] [This method] is highly valued since it fulfils all the desired axioms in measurements of poverty based on consumption and contains a parameter which can be established in accordance with the sensitivity of society towards the distribution of income among the poor.[74]

---

[73] J. Elster, *Local Justice*, p. 4.

[74] PROGRESA, *Más oportunidades para las familias más pobres*, p. 85.

Secondly, PROGRESA, as was stated above, is a focalized program. At present, it is accepted that focalization is the best means of detecting and making available benefits to individuals in a situation of extreme poverty. This method consists in detecting the poorest regions of the country, and, by means of exhaustive family surveys, determining certain values that enable the number of households existing below the extreme poverty line to be established. Focalization contrasts with more universal systems of distribution, such as subsidies, and its apparent advantage lies in the fact that:

> The method aims at ensuring that the means for combating poverty reach effectively those who most need them and that they are articulated comprehensively in order to achieve the full benefit sought [...] Focalization aims not only at efficiency, but also manifests itself in a principle of equity. In view of the fact that resources for fighting poverty, in the best of circumstances, will inevitably be in short supply, it is essential to ensure that those who most need them are benefited, and that they are not directed at people who already receive other means of support or are not in a truly desperate situation.[75]

Amartya Sen, who has proposed methods for measuring poverty and solutions for fighting it, recognizes certain advantages in focalization, such as getting the most out of resources; he has, however, also noted certain problems that arise when applying it.[76] I shall here mention only a few. A fine-tuned method of focalization requires much and highly varied information and thus runs the risk of invading the privacy of individuals; it may also lead to those interviewed distorting information in order to receive the benefit offered; likewise, the identification of people as poor can lead to problems of stigmatization; lastly, men and women characterized as in living extreme poverty may come to feel that they are regarded as passive human beings incapable of making decisions.

The invasion of privacy, stigmatization and the vision of the possible beneficiaries as passive individuals takes us back to the ethical concept of poverty, and thus to the primary good defined by Rawls as the social basis of self-respect.

So far we have considered some characteristics of poverty. We have examined various conceptions based on the economic point of

---

[75] CONPROGRESA, *Lineamientos Generales para la Operación del Programa de Educación, Salud y Alimentación*, p. 9.
[76] See A. Sen, "The Political Economy of Targeting", pp. 11–23.

view. We have also taken into account the concept of respect which is intimately involved in the lack of self-esteem that poverty can generate. Finally, a program implemented in Mexico in the late 1990s has been referred to along with some of its problems.

As has already been mentioned briefly, PROGRESA avails itself of certain criteria for distribution: needs, capacities, preferences and consumption. For this reason, the following chapter will examine the most important arguments regarding the criteria for distribution.

II

CRITERIA OF DISTRIBUTION

> Légalité n'est donc que la proportionnalité, et elle
> n'existera d'une manière véritable que lorsque chacun,
> d'après la loi écrite en quelque sorte dans son organisa-
> tion par Dieu lui-même, PRODUIRA SELON SES FA-
> CULTÉS ET CONSOMMERA SELON SES BESOINS.[1]
>
> Louis Blanc, *Organisation du Travail*[1]

INTRODUCTION

When we speak of poverty in the context of theories of distributive justice, the subject that takes on most importance is to have a notion of what governs distribution and, given that goods and services are in scarce supply, what criteria we ought to adopt if we wish to effect a redistribution. Robert Nozick refers to "patterns" of distribution, the notion of a pattern being expressed by what which fills the empty space in the phrase "to each according to his...".[2] This space has been filled by a wide array of concepts: for example merit, needs, capabilities, historical entitlement, etc. This chapter will examine those most discussed at present.

In philosophy, as has already been mentioned, discussion regarding distributive justice was given new impetus by the writings of Rawls. I shall begin, then, by referring to the concept of primary goods, which Rawls regards as of the utmost importance when dealing with the question of distribution.

PRIMARY GOODS

As was mentioned in the first chapter, the Rawlsean conception of justice sets out from the idea that to establish a well-ordered society, assuming the conditions he refers to as the "veil of ignorance", indi-

---

[1] Quoted by John Rawls in "Reply to Alexander and Musgrave", p. 252. "Equality, then, is simply proportionality, and will only truly exist when everybody, in accordance with the law written in some way by God in his organization, produces according to his capacities and consumes according to his needs".

[2] See R. Nozick, *Anarchy, State and Utopia*, p. 159–160.

viduals would, if they were rational, choose the following principles of justice:

1. Each person has an equal right to the most extensive scheme of equal basic liberties compatible with a similar scheme of liberties for all.
2. Social and economic inequalities are to satisfy two conditions: they must be (a) to the greatest benefit of the least advantaged members of society; and (b) attached to offices and positions open to all under conditions of fair equality of opportunity. [3]

Rawls goes on to specify that

> part (a) of the second principle requires certain specifications of the notions of advantage and benefit of the least advantaged in order that the notion of the benefit of the least advantaged be fully explicit. In their general form these specifications assign weights to certain of the primary goods, and citizens' fair shares of those goods are specified by an index which uses these weights. [4]

As I have already mentioned, these goods are:

> …things which it is supposed a rational man wants whatever else he wants. Regardless of what an individual's rational plans are in detail, it is assumed that there are various things which he would prefer more of rather than less. With more of these goods men can generally be assured of greater success in carrying out their intentions and in advancing their ends, whatever these ends may be. [5]

Rawls classifies the primary goods under the following five headings:

1. First, the basic liberties, as given by a list, for example: freedom of thought and liberty of conscience; freedom of association; and the freedom defined by the liberty and integrity of the person, as well as by the rule of law; and finally the political liberties;
2. Second, freedom of movement and choice of occupation against a background of diverse opportunities;
3. Third, powers and prerogatives of offices and positions of responsibility, particularly those in the main political and economic institutions;
4. Fourth, income and wealth; and
5. Finally, the social bases of self-respect.6

---

[3] J. Rawls, "Social Unity and Primary Goods", p. 362.

[4] Loc. cit.

[5] J. Rawls, *Theory of Justice*, p. 92.

[6] J. Rawls, "Social Unity and Primary Goods", in *Collected Papers*, pp. 362–363.

According to Rawls, the "difference principle"—that any economic and social inequalities that exist have to be for the greater benefit of the less favored members of society—introduces "a simplification for the basis of interpersonal comparisons, since such comparisons are made in terms of the expectations of primary social goods". Rawls defines "these expectations simply as the index of these goods which a representative individual can look forward to".[7] He sees primary goods as intimately connected with "a certain conception of the person which leads in turn to a certain conception of social unity".[8] He regards individuals as moral persons,

> moved by two highest-order interests, namely, the interests to exercise the two powers of moral personality. These two powers are the capacity for a sense of right and justice (the capacity to honor fair terms of cooperation), and the capacity to decide upon, to revise and rationally to pursue a conception of the good. Moral persons also have a higher-order (as opposed to a highest-order) interest in advancing their determinate conceptions of the good...[9]

On the other hand, Rawls thinks that primary goods can explain social unity, since while they may well reveal opposed and incommensurable conceptions of the good held by the citizens, a public understanding is possible of what is regarded as beneficial in matters of justice. This means, in his own words, that

> we can actually provide a scheme of basic equal liberties which, when made part of the political constitution [...] ensures for all citizens the development and exercise of their highest-order interests, provided that certain all-purpose means are fairly assured for everyone.[10]

Finally, we may mention that Rawls does not conceive primary goods as a means to psychological well-being; neither are they indicators of the maximization of satisfiers. Primary goods are "social background conditions and all-purpose means generally necessary for forming and rationally pursuing a conception of the good".[11]

---

[7] J. Rawls, *Theory of Justice*, p. 92.
[8] J. Rawls, "Social Unity and Primary Goods", p. 359.
[9] Ibid., p. 365.
[10] Ibid., p. 367.
[11] Ibid., p. 370.

The Rawlsean notion of primary goods as a criterion for distribution has undergone a number of criticisms. Sen, for example notes two problems with Rawls' proposal. The first lies in its homogenizing the individuals receiving the primary goods, since people in fact have very different needs, which change with their state of health, their longevity, climatic conditions, geographical region, working conditions, temperament, even the size of their bodies (which affects their food and clothing needs). This difference between individuals, communities and societies is fundamental for the study of schemas of distribution in poor countries. A theory of justice must evaluate diversity, both among individuals and the social environments in which they live. Thus to judge levels of advantage exclusively on the basis of primary goods leads to a partially sighted morality, since it overlooks differences which may be morally significant.[12] The second problem that Sen notes is that the primary goods have no value in themselves, possessing, rather, an instrumental and intrinsic value.[13] Jon Elster has also pointed out that primary goods are not homogenous but multidimensional, and this entails consequences for theory. On the one hand, a theory must be capable of establishing ordinal comparisons of the groups of primary goods that individuals possess. On the other, some pairs of groups may not be comparable. One group may be higher as regards earnings and the other as regards self-respect. If Rawls does not propose a common criterion serving to measure all the groups, his theory will be indeterminate.[14] Another problem with Rawlsean theory is that it overlooks some of the basic needs, such as those pertaining to health. As for medical and sanitary needs, Rawls tells us: "I put this difficult problem aside [...] and assume that all citizens have physical and psychological capacities within a certain normal range".[15]

Notwithstanding criticism of Rawls, two of the primary goods, income and well-being and the social bases of self-respect, have been useful for detecting levels of poverty, as was outlined in the first chapter.

---

[12] A. Sen, "Equality of What?", p. 158.

[13] In several works, Sen refers to the concept of "primary-goods fetishism", reflecting Marx's idea of "commodity fetishism". Cf. "Equality of What?", p. 158, and "Capability and Well-being".

[14] See J. Elster, *Local justice*, p. 227.

[15] J. Rawls, "Social Unity and Primary Goods", p. 168.

NEEDS

One of the most important, and therefore, most discussed criteria of distribution is, beyond doubt, that of needs. The attraction of this criterion lies in its providing an objective basis for distribution which does not depend on the wishes, preferences or values of individuals. Perhaps our intuitions regarding poverty might bring us to the consideration that, in places where this reaches extreme conditions, it is indispensable to talk of needs, for if these are not met, it is doubtful that any policy aimed at combating poverty will succeed.

In many discussions regarding distributive justice, recurrence to the concept of needs as a criterion for distribution of certain goods and services is associated with Marx's celebrated assertion in his critique of the *Gotha Program*: "from each according to his abilities, to each according to his needs".[16] Nonetheless, it is important to point out that this concept has also been studied by the so-called "equalitarian" liberal theorists,[17] whose discussions are even more interesting and which—unlike the Marxist principle postulated against a background of abundance—incorporate the problem of scarcity. But before continuing it is important to clarify that we shall refer only to the concept of basic needs, since in a broader treatment, which would include instrumental needs, we would be obliged to distinguish not only between the concept of desires or wishes on the one hand and needs on the other, but also between needs and wants, or needs and interests.[18] These distinctions become relevant when we deal with the subject of "well-being", since, while subjective well-being refers to what people want or desire, objective well-being refers to what people need.

Several philosophers have tried to provide a definition or a list of basic needs. What they attempt to do is, in some cases, to define a concept of need which is not relative, and in others to provide a list of basic needs that can be compatible with certain cultural variations. First we shall refer to two attempts to define the basic needs and, later to two authors who propose lists.

---

[16] On Marx's theory of needs, see A. Heller, *The Theory of Needs in Marx*.

[17] In particular: Bernard Williams, "The Idea of Equality", pp. 230–249; and A. Wagstaff, E. van Doorslaer, and F. Rutten, "Introduction", p. 10.

[18] See the discussion of this latter distinction in M. Platts, *Moral Realities*, pp. 34–38, and D. Wiggins, "Claims of Needs", pp. 159–161.

TWO DEFINITIONS OF NEEDS

David Wiggins[19] maintains that the objectivity of basic needs is compatible with the incorporation of certain individual, historical and cultural differences, since what is required is to establish a threshold of satisfaction of needs which admits variation. Now, Wiggins's characterization of needs aims to go beyond the recognition of a threshold in order to establish what those basic needs are. He points to five elements that characterize a need: 1) "badness", which refers to the degree of harm that a person suffers if the good in question is not provided to him; 2) the "consequential question of urgency", which relate to the degree of soonness with which the good must be provided if harm is not to ensue; 3) the "basicness", which refers to the degree to which our reasons for excluding future scenarios in which a person would remain unharmed without the good in question, are based on laws of nature, environmental and invariable laws, or facts regarding the human constitution; 4) "entrenchment", which refers to the degree of feasibility of having some other good accepted as a substitute for the one in question; 5) "substitutability", which refers to the degree of possibility of weakening the claims of need by arranging for one good to be replaced by another.

A need that is urgent, that demands satisfaction if harmful consequences are to be avoided, that is basic, entrenched, and irreplaceable is an objective need that programs of social justice must attend to. An example of a basic need is the amount of calories and proteins that an individual must consume (2,082 calories and 35.1 grams of proteins a day) in order to maintain health and development. The consumption of calories and proteins fulfills the requirements indicated by Wiggins, i.e. that in all possible worlds where the same laws of nature, the same environmental conditions and a particular human constitution obtain, human beings would suffer harm if they failed to consume the minimum quantity of calories and proteins mentioned above. According to Wiggins, to characterize basic needs in this way is to conceive of the concept of need as "a modal concept of a special kind which imports the linked ideas of a situation and a non-negotiable (or in-the-circumstances-non-negotiable) good that *together* leave no alternative but to…".[20]

---

[19] See D. Wiggins, loc. cit.
[20] Ibid., p. 167.

James Griffin, on the other hand, relates needs to an objective conception of well-being. This means that basic needs have a priority over wishes and one may not regard the former as a subgroup of the latter.

According to Griffin, *to need*, unlike *to desire*, is not an "intentional verb"; it is only possible to need something when something identical will do just as well. The particular significance of needs lies in their being "not tied to a subject's perception of the object". Now two kinds of needs exist: instrumental and basic needs. The former serve as means to attain certain purposes. The latter are ours simply because we are human beings. For example, in order to live we need to eat, and survival forms part of human existence. Basic needs are also absolute; human beings need food simply to survive and not in order to achieve some other goal. The aims pursued by satisfying basic needs are self-evident: survival, health, avoidance of harm and proper functioning.[21]

Now, the notions health, damage and proper functioning are too vague to explain needs. Moreover, there are certain needs that are more difficult to explain as basic: an example of these is education. Nonetheless, Griffin believes that it is possible to think in terms of a more restricted concept. This concept might be that of "minimum provision". Human beings need, for their lives to be worth while, a minimum of resources, of liberty, rest and education. If we pay attention to the notion of minimum provision it is in order to maintain that basic needs are those conditions necessary in order to reach a goal. Basic needs are not what human beings desire but what allow them to lead and develop a human life.[22]

Now the authors I have mentioned admit that the concept of needs may be an indeterminate one, and that it has a considerable conventional content. Nevertheless, they believe that, although the line between the basic and the non-basic may change from one society to another, a certain rationality exists that allows us to fix a line between them. This affirmation is of great importance for those countries in which extreme poverty exists, and so to speak of needs relative to the social context may be irresponsible. Thus, according to

---

[21] See James Griffin, *Well-Being*, p. 41.
[22] Ibid., p. 43.

Griffin, when we refer to basic needs we do not have to interpret, but merely to stipulate.[23]

THE LIST OF BASIC NEEDS

In view of the indeterminacy of the concept of needs *per se*, there are authors who prefer to specify a list of items without which a life would cease to be human.

There can be no doubt that the person who has most strongly defended this position is Martha Nussbaum. The importance of her thinking lies in its sets out from what she calls "an internal essentialist position". This position enables her to postulate the existence of characteristics common to all individuals, enabling us to specify a set of basic needs that do not depend on historical, cultural and social circumstances.[24]

In support of her position she appeals to the following two facts as her starting point:

> …first, that we do recognize others as human beings across many divisions of time and place. Whatever the differences we encounter, we are rarely in doubt as to when we are dealing with a human being or when we are not. […] Second, we do have a broadly shared general consensus about the features whose absence means the end of a human form of life.[25]

According to Nussbaum, the internal-essentialist position takes account of the most important functions of human beings. Once these are identified, it is possible to study ways in which social policies can be directed towards them. Internal-essentialism sets out from the idea that human beings can be seen "from within" and that it is possible to distinguish in them what is "indispensable in our lives" and what is accidental.[26]

Nussbaum is aware that internal essentialism faces three objections: the first has to do with essentialism's characteristic neglect of historical and cultural differences. According to this objection, the only way to distinguish what there is of essential in human beings

---

[23] Ibid., p. 45.
[24] See M. Nussbaum, "Human Functioning and Social Justice: A Defense of Aristotelian Essentialism", pp. 203–246.
[25] Ibid., p. 215.
[26] Ibid., pp. 207–208.

from the purely accidental is by consensus and, given that generally such consensus does not exist, it is necessary to have recourse to some authority. The second objection concerns the abandonment of the concept of autonomy. Some authors who belong to the liberal tradition think that essentialism constitutes an impediment to stipulating that individuals must choose the life plan that suits them best. The third objection refers to the prejudices that may arise in the application of certain policies. For example, if we operate with a particular conception of human beings which has some normative bearing on our moral or political decisions, we shall have to decide who are the beings who fall within that conception. This objection is based on the fact that throughout history theories have been upheld that leave certain groups outside the human: for example, even Aristotle excluded women and slaves,[27] and in recent times the Jews were excluded by Nazi ideology.

Nussbaum accepts the criticism made against a type of essentialism—metaphysical essentialism. That is to say, she accepts the criticism of a philosophical conception that regards the world in a predetermined manner, regardless of the subject who knows it, and which thus makes a sharp distinction between the world of facts and that of values. This kind of philosophical conception holds that objective and scientific explanations are totally distinct from moral or political explanations. Nussbaum accepts certain philosophical positions such as those of Sen and Putnam, who maintain that it is not possible to make such a distinction between facts and values, since when we decide what counts as a fact we are already making a value judgment. While she accepts that many internal essentialist positions have been arrogant, overlooking the distinction between different cultures and ways of life, and ignoring the choices of individuals and the exercise of their autonomy, she believes that in the essentialism that she proposes a space exists for autonomy and for the postulation of the need of individuals for possibilities to carry out their life plans. Her aim is to offer a normative list of what she considers essential items for conceptualizing what a human life is. While she accepts that such lists are necessarily vague, she holds that it is better to "be vaguely than precisely wrong".

Her list (somewhat paraphrased) is as follows:

---

[27] Ibid., p. 209.

Mortality: All human beings face death. At the same time all human beings feel repugnance towards death.

The human body: We spend our whole lives inside a particular body, whose possibilities and whose vulnerability do not make us members of one human society rather than another. These bodies, which are much more similar than dissimilar to each other, open up to us certain options and deny us others, give us certain needs and also certain possibilities for virtue. Of course the experience of the body is culturally configured, but the body itself has needs that do not change and which establish the limit of what can be accepted, thus ensuring a high degree of coincidence.

1. *Hunger and thirst: the need for food and drink.* All human beings need to eat and drink in order to live; all have comparable, although varying, nutritional requirements. Likewise all human beings have appetites that are indicators of this need.
2. *The need for shelter.* A recurrent theme in all myths about mankind is the nakedness of human beings, their relative susceptibility to heat, cold, and the ravages of the elements.
3. *Sexual desire.* Although less urgent than the need for food, drink and shelter (in the sense that one can live without satisfying them), sexual needs and desires are characteristics of practically all human life.
4. *Mobility.* The form of life of human beings is constituted in part by their capacity for moving from place to place.

Capacity for pleasure and pain. The experiences of pleasure and pain are common to all human life.

Cognitive capability: perceiving, imagining and thinking. All human beings have sense perception, the ability to imagine, think, make distinctions and (As Aristotle puts it in *Metaphysics* I.1) to "reach out for understanding", and these capabilities are of fundamental importance.

Early infant development. All human beings start life as hungry babies, aware of their helplessness, experiencing how the closeness and distance of the person or persons on whom they depend alternates.

Practical reason. All human beings aim to participate in planning and directing their own lives, posing and answering questions regarding what is good and how one ought to live.

Affiliation with other human beings. We define ourselves in terms of at lest two kinds of affiliation: intimate family and personal relations, and social or civic relations.

Relatedness to other species and nature. Human beings recognize that they are not the only living beings on the planet, that they are animals living alongside other animals.

Humor and play. All human life makes room for recreation and laughter.

Separation. However much we live with and for others, each of us is "one in number", who walks along an individual path through the world, from birth to death.[28]

The list includes two elements: limits and capabilities. A life without those capacities would be too poor to be lived. The problem of limits is more complicated since human life, in general, can be defined as the struggle to transcend those limits. No human being wishes to undergo hunger, feel pain or die.

According to Nussbaum, there are two thresholds that allow us to characterize a life as human: the first is that of the capabilities for functioning; when people's lives are below this threshold they cannot be called human. The second represents a level below which functions are reduced to the extent that, though we may still regard such a life as human, we could not consider it a "good" life. The second threshold is the one that is important for the devising of public policies since it is hardly acceptable that these be aimed merely at ensuring a society which reaches the minimum threshold.

Nussbaum's opinion is that any public legislation and planning ought to foster development of the following possibilities:

1. Being able to live to the end a complete human life, as far as it is possible; not dying prematurely, or before one's life is so reduced as to be not worth living.
2. Being able to have good health; to be adequately nourished; to have adequate shelter; having opportunities for sexual satisfaction; being able to move from place to place.
3. Being able to avoid unnecessary and non-beneficial pain, and to have pleasurable experiences.
4. Being able to use the five senses, being able to imagine, to think and to reason.
5. Being able to have attachments to things and persons outside ourselves; to love those who love and care for us, to grieve at their absence; in general, to love, grieve, to feel longing and gratitude.
6. Being able to form a conception of the good and to engage in critical reflection about the planning of our own lives.
7. Being able to live for and with others, to recognize and show concern for other human beings, to engage in various forms of familial and social interaction.
8. Being able to live with concern for and in relation to animals, plants, and the world of nature.
9. Being able to laugh, to play, to enjoy recreational activities.
10. Being able to live one's own life and nobody else's; being able to live one's own life in one's very own surroundings and context.[29]

---

[28] Ibid., pp. 216–220.

According to Nussbaum any public policy which aims at promoting the good of human beings must have as its goal the realizing of these possibilities.[30]

Nussbaum replies to the above-mentioned critiques of internal essentialism. First, she thinks that the reference to the absence of historical conditions is unwarranted, since the list is "thick and vague" enough to incorporate cultural and social differences. Secondly— with regard to the neglect of essentialist positions for the autonomy of persons—she states that her own essentialism does not assume that the State should foster citizens' acting in particular ways, but rather, that it should ensure that all human beings have the resources and the conditions necessary to act as best they see fit and that opportunities be effectively available.[31] Finally, regarding the third criticism, if we adopt an internal essentialist position, we shall not— according to Nussbaum—be able to establish a "normative" scale of values regarding human beings.

Another author who offers a list is Len Doyal.[32] He believes that, despite the popularity achieved by some thinkers who deny the existence of basic needs, their postulates are plausible but superficial. Such attempts are popular because of the strong feelings that people have about their basic needs and about the importance of cultural differences in their configuration. He believes, however, that subjective feelings do not constitute a reliable source for attending to demands based on needs. This is because at times we may strongly desire things that do us harm and may ignore things that are necessary to avoid such harm. It is, therefore, essential to accept the idea that the basic needs have an objective and universal basis. An objective basis is that which, both empirically and theoretically, is independent of desires or wishes and subjective preferences. A universal basis means that the harm caused by the absence of a particular good is the same for all human beings.

According to Doyal, the word *need* is used, explicitly or implicitly, to refer to a particular category of goals thought of as universalizable. It is important to stress that in this sense needs are distin-

---

[29] Ibid., p. 222.
[30] Loc. cit.
[31] Ibid., p. 72.
[32] See Len Doyal, "A Theory of Human Need", pp. 157–172.

guished from other goals concerning what people want or wish for and which depend on personal preferences and the cultural environment. Human beings have universal goals which correspond to basic needs and it is necessary to attend to them lest they suffer some specific and objective harm. Thus, according to Doyal, basic needs are universalizable preconditions that, when satisfied, enable people to participate, as actively as possible, in those ways of life that men and women might choose if they had the opportunity to do so.[33]

According to Doyal the basic needs are health and personal autonomy. In order for individuals to be able to act and to be responsible, they must have a particular physical and mental capacity which consists in the possession of a living body governed by all the relevant causal processes; they must, besides, have the mental competency for deliberating and choosing. Competency and the capacity for choice constitute the most basic level of personal autonomy. Thus physical survival and personal autonomy are preconditions for individuals to be able to act, whatever the culture they may belong to. On considering physical health, Doyal concludes that this may be defined negatively, i.e. that without which it would be impossible to have a life expectancy and whose absence would cause the appearance of physical diseases that may be conceptualized in biomedical terms.[34]

Doyal distinguishes three ideas that are indispensable for understanding the notion of personal autonomy. The first refers to the comprehension that people have of themselves, of their culture and what is expected of themselves within it. The second is related to men and women's psychological capacity to create their own options. The third concerns the objective opportunities which permit a person to act or not to act. Autonomy is related intimately to formal education and, according to Doyal, its minimum levels can be described by means of the following characteristics:

- Agents have the intellectual capacity to fix goals in accordance with their lifestyle.
- Agents possess sufficient self-confidence to be able to wish to act and participate in social life.
- Agents are able to formulate consistent purposes and are capable of communicating them to others.
- Agents perceive their actions as their own.

---

[33] Ibid., p. 158.
[34] Ibid., p. 159.

- Agents are capable of understanding the empirical restrictions that impede or prevent the achievement of their goals.
- Agents may feel themselves to be responsible for the decisions they take and for their consequences.[35]

Thus personal autonomy, like health, can be understood negatively: i.e. by stressing the objective harm that would result if the above-mentioned characteristics were not fulfilled. These characteristics are independent of the culture to which men and women belong.

Now returning to the theoretical discussion, it was mentioned above that Nussbaum's defense is of an Aristotelian nature, because it underlines the satisfaction of needs that are basic and essential in order for human beings to realize their potential. Doyal, on the other hand, upholds a Kantian position on stressing the universality of basic needs in their own right.

As may be appreciated, both Nussbaum and Doyal uphold the existence of essential and universalizable basic needs without overlooking individual and cultural differences. The theses put forward by these authors agree in affirming that while essential and universalizable basic needs certainly exist, what may change according to individuals, culture and history is the way of satisfying them.

Like the notion of primary goods, distribution in accordance with needs has received various types of criticism. The first is based on the relative nature of the concepts that appear in the definition, such as well-being and harm, and the second on the tendency for paternalism to manifest itself in policies based on distribution according to needs. It is generally the case that those in charge of implementing public policies are the ones who decide what it is that those aimed at need.

With regard to the relativism of certain concepts, a broad discussion has taken place regarding the different ways of conceiving of and measuring the level of well-being. Nor is it easy to establish the degree of harm suffered by individuals when they lack a certain good. Some authors—Gerry Cohen,[36] for example—have pointed out that human needs are not constant throughout history, since as they evolve through time they generate changes of character and customs.

---

[35] Ibid., p. 160.
[36] See *Karl Marx's Theory of History: a Defence*, p. 103.

On the other hand, society itself also engenders needs, causing even those that would appear to be "natural" to be altered by social usage. For example, as Peter Townsend states:

Any rigorous conceptualization of the social determination of need dissolves the idea of 'absolute' need. And a thorough-going relativity applies to time as well as place. The necessities of life are not fixed. They are continuously being adapted and augmented as changes take place in a society and its products. Increasing stratification and a developing division of labor, as well as the growth of powerful new organizations, create, as well as reconstitute, 'need'. Certainly no standard of sufficiency could be revised only to take account of changes in prices, for that would ignore changes in the goods and services consumed as well as new obligations and expectations placed on members of the community. Lacking an alternative criterion, the best assumption would be to relate sufficiency to the average rise (or fall) in real incomes.[37]

Another criticism of the use of the concept of need concerns the fact of its serving as a justification for paternalistic behavior. We might define a policy as paternalistic when it entails the following three elements: interference in a person's freedom of action, coercion, and the absence of consent; paternalism has been defined as "the interference with a person's liberty of action justified by reasons referring exclusively to the welfare, good, happiness, needs, interests or values of the person being coerced".[38]

The defenders of needs, however, consider that the problem of paternalism seems of less moment when we remember that cases exist where it is justified. For instance, when an individual who is being coerced to receive a good is unaware of the harm that somebody else may suffer in the absence of the good in question. There is also an argument for justifying paternalism based on harms and risks. An example my be illustrative. Let us suppose that a social policy involves effecting a vaccination campaign. The people to whom it is directed refuse to be vaccinated. To justify paternalism it is necessary to take into account the possible harm to be avoided, the risks, and the goals pursued by the community. Social policy will thus have to consider at least the following aspects: *a)* the degree of prob-

---

[37] Quoted by Amartya Sen, "Poor, Relatively Speaking", pp. 327–328.
[38] Gerald Dworkin, "Paternalism", p. 65.

ability of harm; for instance if, in the case of an epidemic, the likelihood of members of the community catching the illness is very high; *b)* the seriousness of the harm compared to the risk of carrying out the paternalistic action; there are cases where the harm caused by the illness may be mortal or irreversible and the application of the vaccine entails no risk; *c)* the knowledge that the objective pursued through a paternalistic action is important for the community; for example, the knowledge that people appreciate health although they reject the means to conserve it; and, *d)* that the paternalistic action is justified as the best option for attaining the proposed goal; i.e. that the vaccine is the best means known for preventing the disease. When we speak about basic needs in particular it is possible to find a multitude of cases of justified paternalism.[39]

The defenders of the criterion of distribution in accordance with needs think that, as what is at stake are goods and services that enable a life to be regarded as a good human life, there should be no objections to allowing instances of paternalism, as long as it can be justified.

PREFERENCES

Against the objectivity of needs, some authors think that any distribution must necessarily be effected according to subjective criteria. Given that individuals have the capacity to choose their life plans and the means that will lead them towards their goals, the appropriate norm for distribution must be the revealed preference. The theory of distributive justice according to preferences would prescribe "to each according to his preferences". This concept arises historically out of that of interest, Already Edgworth in 1881, in his work *Mathematical Psychics*, stated that "the first principle of Economics is that every agent is motivated only by self-interest".[40] The word "self-interest" refers, indisputably, to a concept that was originated by certain seventeenth and eighteenth-century thinkers such as Locke and Hume, and was later taken up by Jeremy Bentham and John Stuart Mill as the concept of utility.

In the nineteenth century, philosophers and economists referred to utility as an indicator of the overall well-being of individuals, as an

---

[39] See Joel Feinberg, *Social Philosophy*, p. 45.
[40] Cited by A. Sen, "Rational Fools", p. 87.

indicator of the pleasure generated by the obtaining of something that was desired. They conceived of utility as a numerical measure of a person's happiness, and deduced that individuals made choices in order to maximize their utility, in other words in order to be as happy as possible.

Due to certain conceptual problems such as the assigning of a measure of utility associated with different choices, philosophers and economists sought to disconnect the concept of utility from that of happiness. Mills' famous phrase "it is better to be Socrates dissatisfied than a pig satisfied" only created perplexity. It does not actually clarify why we should assign more value to the unsatisfied desires of Socrates than the satisfied ones of a pig. Utility, instead of being related to happiness, became linked to the concept of preference. This facilitates the following psychological assumption: if we observe that a person prefers a good x and rejects y, we can claim that she has shown her preference for x over y. Preferences may be represented numerically, assigning a higher value to the preferred alternative. Given these characteristics, any action can be interpreted in the light of the maximization of utility and, for a choice to be rational, all that is necessary is consistency. A choice is consistent when the following rules are applied:

1. Preferences must be complete. This means that certain goods can be compared and that an individual can choose between them.
2. Preferences must be reflexive. This means that one good is at least as good as another.
3. Preferences must be transitive. This means that if an agent thinks that x is at least as good as y and y is at least as good as z, then x must be at least as good as z.[41]

The advantage of this kind of approach is that it allows us to express numerically and graphically a series of choices that explain to us the behavior of human beings; in the same way it opens the door for us to assign a numerical value to the utility that individuals derive from the acquisition of a particular good. Unlike the criterion of needs, preferences are subjective. Nothing is harmful or favorable unless it is experienced by someone as such.

According to Amartya Sen, the popularity of this approach is due to the confluence of "an obsessive concern with observability and a

---

[41] See, for example, J. Elster, "Introduction".

peculiar belief that choice (in particular, market choice) is the only human aspect that can be observed".[42] For example, many studies of poverty are based on income and above all on consumption, since these are regarded as empirically verifiable data.

There is no doubt that the theory of preferences avoids some of the problems that we found in distribution according to needs, since a person chooses what is most to her liking, and thus we avoid paternalism. It also gets around the problem of relativism, since the preference approach enables us to include changes in these in societies, culture and history. However, this theory too is not without problems of its own. One of these is the information required to exercise preferences adequately.[43] In the case of calories and proteins, for example, individuals may choose foodstuffs that lack these elements, as a result of lacking adequate information regarding what foods provide them. Another problem is that it only measures the result of choices from an ordinal point of view, in other words, we may know that a person prefers x to y but without knowing the degree of preference. Perhaps the most serious problem for the subject that concerns us is the impossibility of making interpersonal comparisons, which could lead us to maintain that a situation in which a person is forced to chose between a piece of bread and a tortilla is comparable, in terms of justice, to one in which the choice is between an excellent Burgundy or a first-class Rioja. Thus, Martha Nussbaum remarks that to concentrate very narrowly

...on subjective expressions of satisfaction brings with it a number of serious problems. First of all, desires and subjective preferences are not always reliable indices of what a person really needs [...]. Desires and satisfactions are highly malleable. The rich and pampered easily become accustomed to their luxury and view with pain and frustration a life in which they are treated just like everyone else. The poor and deprived frequently adjust their expectations and aspirations to the low level of life they have known; thus their failure to express dissatisfaction may often be a sign that they really do have enough. This is all the more true when the deprivations in question include deprivation of education and other in-

---

[42] Amartya Sen, *The Standard of Living*, p. 12.
[43] See Dan Brock, "Quality of Life Measures in Health Care and Medical Ethics", in M. Nussbaum and A. Sen, *The Quality of Life*, 96–97.

formation about alternative ways of life. Circumstances confine the imagination.[44]

Another author who has criticized the notion of distribution based exclusively on preferences is Ronald Dworkin.[45] He proposes under the heading of "equality of resources" a distinction which is of great importance for a theory of distribution.[46] He states that differences exist that generate in individuals inequality arising from the exercise of their preferences, but also from the circumstances in which these find themselves. Among such circumstances appear, principally, the environment, the social context and genetic inheritance. Dworkin understands by resources not only material goods which can be exchanged on the market but also talents and genetic disadvantages or those due to an accident. He distinguishes between "brute bad luck", when the consequences of an action do not depend on individuals, and optional luck which results from the "gambles" that people make consciously. Equality of resources depends on establishing a market system, limited by taxes, which would be justified as the distribution resulting from the equal possibility that members may have to insure themselves against the disadvantages that come about from the circumstance in which they find themselves. In Dworkin's words:

> Equality of resources [...] requires essentially a free market in capital, labor and consumption, and it intervenes in such markets not to replace but only to perfect them, either by correcting market imperfections of the kind economists standardly recognize, or by correcting a different kind of imperfection: the failure of actual markets to offer standard forms of insurance on terms that make it equally available to everyone.[47]

Dworkin thinks that the possibility to buy insurance would erase to some extent the distinction between brute and optional fate since it offers citizens the possibility of managing their circumstance without dispensing with their preferences.

Despite criticism of the notion of preference, this may enrich a social policy as long as we include certain evaluative elements. It is

---

[44] M. Nussbaum, "Human Functioning and Social Justice: A Defense of Aristotelian Essentialism", p. 230.

[45] See R. Dworkin, "What Is Equality?, Part 1: Equality of Welfare", pp. 185–246.

[46] See R. Dworkin, "What Is Equality?, Part 2: Equality of Resources", pp. 283–345.

[47] R. Dworkin, "Do Liberty and Equality Conflict?", pp. 53–54.

important to take into account individuals' preferences, not only because we can observe them, but also because through the exercise of such preferences, individuals are able to evaluate the possibilities presented to them and to accept responsibility for their choices. What we may thus lose in precision is compensated for by an unquestionable gain in application. On the other hand, we could fuse the notion of preferences to that of autonomy alluded to by Doyal. In this way the possibility of exercising a preference—even if a minimal one, as in the cases of extreme poverty—would be equivalent to an exercise in autonomy.

CAPABILITIES

A very important notion when we discuss modes of distribution is one invented by Amartya Sen: the concept of *capabilities*. This provides us with a middle term between the subjectivity of preferences and the objectivity of needs.

For Sen equality is the possibility of developing certain capabilities and certain "functionings", and he defends an idea of liberty which is both negative and positive; he is interested not only in what people *must* do but in what they *can* do and *can* be.[48] Now, by the word "functioning" Sen understands the elements constitutive of a life. A functioning is an achievement of a person, what she is capable of doing and being. By capability he understands the freedom a person has to choose between different ways of life.[49] Likewise, he contemplates the need for a type of evaluation that would allow us to select the kind of functioning and the type of capabilities human beings need and must acquire. In order to clarify the difference between his proposal based on capabilities and the Rawlsean distribution of primary goods, Sen makes use of the following example. He asks us to think of a good like rice, for instance, and highlights four fundamental aspects: first, the notion of the *good* itself (rice); secondly the *characteristic* of the good (it nourishes and provides calories); thirdly, the notion of the *functioning* of a person (living without deficiency of calories); and fourthly, the notion of *utility* of the good

---

[48] The concept of capability leads us back to a concept regarding human beings that, as we shall see below, is of key importance for understanding Sen's thought: that of *agency*.
[49] See A. Sen, *The Standard of Living*, op. cit., p. 29.

(the use of rice, the pleasure given by its consumption or the satisfied desire that arises from the functioning related to the characteristics of rice).[50] When the accent is put on the third aspect, i.e. on the functioning of a person, something uniquely important is being indicated; the traditional point of view on positive liberty is interpreted in terms of the capabilities an agent has to function in life. These capabilities condition what a person can do and be.

Sen insists on the distinction between the four above-mentioned aspects. Three of these characteristics are an abstraction from goods and refer more to these than to persons. In contrast, functioning addresses what a person can do with them. While the characteristics of the goods a person possesses are related to the capabilities that person acquires—since the person acquires capabilities using and consuming such goods—we must distinguish between characteristics and capabilities. If we value the ability of a person to function without nutritional deficiencies, we will tend to favor those arrangements in which people acquire foods rich in nutrients. In this way we are not valuing the good in itself, but in relation with the functioning it facilitates. For Sen, the property of the goods and their corresponding characteristics are instrumental and contingent, and only acquire relevance to the extent that they help us attain what we value, namely capabilities.

Thus we may approach capabilities via the functionings attained (what a person is actually capable of doing) or of the group of alternatives she has (her real opportunities). Sen explains that "if the extent of such functioning enjoyed by a person can be represented by a real number, then [her] actual achievement is given by a functioning vector in an n-dimensional space of n functionings (presuming finiteness of distinct functionings). The set of alternative functioning vectors available to her for choice is called her capability set".[51]

In this Sen takes his inspiration from Isaiah Berlin, who apart from explaining the idea of negative freedom as restriction, develops the concept of positive liberty. Berlin says:

> The 'positive' sense of the word 'liberty' derives from the wish on the part of the individual to be his own master. I wish my life and decisions to depend on myself, not on external forces of whatever kind. I wish to be the instrument of my

---

[50] A. Sen, "Rights and Capabilities", p. 138.
[51] Cf. A. Sen, *On Economic Inequality*, p. 200.

own, not of other men's acts of will. I wish to be a subject, not an object; to be moved by reasons, by conscious purposes which are my own, not by causes which affect me, as it were, from outside. I wish to be somebody, not nobody; a doer—deciding, not being decided for, self-directed and not acted upon by external nature or by other men as if I were a thing, or an animal, or a slave incapable of playing a human role, that is of conceiving goals and policies of my own and realizing them.[52]

Sen analyzes Berlin's concept of liberty and makes the following observations: liberty is a matter both of opportunities and processes. Opportunities involve not only the ability to get the best within a range of possibilities, but also to the spectrum of possibilities offered. Processes, on the other hand, refer to people's freedom of decision and imply the field of autonomy of individual choices and their immunity to the interference of others.[53] He identifies thus three facets of the concept of freedom: a) opportunity to obtain something; b) autonomy of decisions; and c) immunity to intrusions. There is no problem about including a concept of liberty as autonomy of persons and immunity to intrusions in the market as a system of distribution, but there are serious difficulties when we try to incorporate the *opportunity* to obtain something; the market is a system which only with difficulty can be made to incorporate the whole set of valuable options that individuals have and which allow them to choose a subset of functionings—what each person is capable of doing—and which in fact configure their ways of life.[54]

A notion inseparable from the concept of capabilities and functionings is that of well-being, since this forms one of the objective principles of a distributive policy. Sen tells us that "in order to find an adequate conception of well-being it is necessary to avoid two dangers which arise from different directions. One of these consists in adopting a basically subjective conception in terms of one or other of the means of utility as a mental state".[55] As we have already seen, while happiness and the satisfaction of desires have undoubtedly some value, our motivations tend to be much more complex. The other danger consists in feeling ourselves attracted by an objective

---

[52] I. Berlin, "Two Concepts of Liberty", p. 149.

[53] See A. Sen, *Bienestar, justicia y mercado*, p. 132 (the Spanish translation of *Welfare, Justice and Market* used as the original was not available).

[54] See Damián Salcedo, "Introducción", p. 33.

[55] A. Sen, *Bienestar, justicia y mercado*, p. 75.

(and in some sense impersonal) direction, on seeking a criterion which is not clouded by circumstantial contingencies. Sen understands by an objective criterion of a person's well-being the parameter which enables us to appreciate the said well-being independently of tastes and interests. The difficulty of finding an objective criterion is due to the variety of characteristics of different individuals, cultures and societies. Despite this difficulty, he believes that a value can be assigned to certain personal, social or cultural characteristics that are not susceptible to parametrical incorporation in a function of evaluation.[56] This becomes clear when we consider basic capabilities like food, education, health, housing, etc. On the one hand, on recognizing personal and cultural diversity, Sen distances himself from positions that adopt universal distribution criteria; on the other, by acknowledging certain objective criteria he also takes a distance from relativist positions.

According to Sen, we can conceive of well-being in terms of what is available to a person in order to increase her functionings. The latter do not only include activities (like eating, reading or seeing), but also states of existence or of being: for instance, being well-nourished, not having malaria, not feeling ashamed on account of one's poor clothing or worn-out footwear. Well-being is tied to the set of activities or states of existence that a person really achieves, in other words, the *functioning vector*. Thus the fundamental characteristic of a person's well-being is the functioning vector that she can attain. The various functioning vectors can in turn be evaluated by individuals or societies.[57]

For Sen, however, the study of problems of distribution not only requires us to consider the "well-being achievement", but also "well-being freedom".[58] If, as we live, the sense of freedom remits to the opportunity individuals have for obtaining the things they value, then liberty for a person's well-being refers to her possibility of enjoying the functionings that are within her capabilities. Thus, for this author, freedom is related to well-being, since the increase in a person's

---

[56] Ibid., p. 75.
[57] Ibid., p. 77.
[58] See A. Sen, "Capability and Well-Being", pp. 36 ff.; and *Bienestar, justicia y mercado*, p. 83.

freedom is directly related with the quantity and quality of the options presented to her.

Another fundamental concept in Sen's work—one that is related to the idea of capability—is that of agency. The freedom of well-being is a concept centered on the capability of a person to have a number of functionings and to enjoy the consequent results of well-being. The idea of liberty as well-being of the person is part of her liberty as agency. "Freedom to be agents" refers to what a person is at liberty to do and obtain in the search for goals and the values that she may consider important. The agent facet of a person cannot be understood without taking into account her objectives, purposes, fidelities, obligations and—in the broad sense—her conception of good. The freedom to be an agent is the freedom to obtain what a person regards as valuable.[59]

The idea of agency is fundamental for understanding what, according to Sen, must be taken into account by social policies. Any method for distributing scarce resources, above all in situations where extreme poverty exists, most regard beneficiaries as active agents, as individuals capable of setting themselves goals and seeking the most appropriate means to attain them. For this reason, he criticizes so strongly those theories and policies that regard people who find themselves in a situation of poverty as passive beings unable to take their own decisions.[60]

An important point, particularly for poor countries, is raised by Sen's study of basic capabilities—i.e. those that enable us to fulfill minimally the most crucial and important functionings. The identification of the minimum acceptable levels of certain basic capabilities (below which it is considered that people suffer scandalous privations) may provide a focus on poverty. One of the most significant elements of Sen's work is, in fact, his appreciation of the capacities for detecting extreme poverty, criticizing at the same time those definitions based on income and consumption.[61]

Most studies of poverty set out on the basis of inequality of income and consumption; Sen, on the other hand, stresses that while these are certainly factors affecting the opportunities people have,

---

[59] Ibid., p. 86.
[60] See A. Sen, "The Political Economy of Targeting", pp. 11–23.
[61] See A. Sen, "Capability and Well-Being", pp. 41 ff.

they are in no way the only ones. For example, one person may be richer than another in terms of income and yet suffer from an incurable disease, and thus have to spend most of his salary on medical attention. The real opportunities enjoyed by individuals are substantially affected by their particular circumstances (age, disability, proneness to illness, special talents, gender, maternity, etc.), and by the characteristics of the environment in which they live (epidemiological conditions, extent of pollution, prevalence of local crime, etcetera).[62]

Poverty is, for Sen, the deprivation of capabilities. He of course recognizes the existence of "wide agreement that poverty exists when a person lacks the real opportunity of avoiding hunger or undernourishment or homelessness". Clearly, an inadequate income strongly impedes the development of capabilities, but Sen goes beyond this. He sums up his own position in the following points:

(1) poverty can be sensibly *defined* in terms of capability deprivation (the connection with lowness of income is only instrumental);

(2) there are influences on capability deprivation *other* than lowness of income; and,

(3) the instrumental relation between low income and low capabilities is *parametrically variable* between different communities and even between different families and different individuals.[63]

These parametrical variations can be explained by various reasons. First, the relation between income and capabilities is affected by people's ages (the particular needs of children and old people), by gender and social roles (the special responsibilities of maternity and diverse obligations imposed by uses and customs), by the kind of locality one lives in (the insecurity and violence of some urban environments), by the degree of exposure to epidemics, and by other variants over which people have little or no control.

Second, there may be a "coupling of disadvantages between (1) income deprivation and (2) adversity in converting income into functionings". The consequences of old age and sickness reduce not only the capacity for earning money, but also hamper the conversion of income into capabilities, since income is inevitably deflected into

---

[62] See A. Sen, *On Economic Inequality*, p. 195.
[63] Ibid., p. 211.

the costs of assistance, treatment, etc.) before such a person's functionings can be raised to something closer to those of a young and healthy person. "This entails that 'real poverty' (in terms of capability deprivation) may be, in a significant sense, more intense than what appears in the income space".

Third, distribution within families is more complex than what one might imagine if one considers only overall family income. This overlooks cases where, for example, distribution shows a marked preference for boys in detriment to girls.

Fourth, "*relative* privation in terms of *incomes* can yield *absolute* deprivation in terms of *capabilities*". For various reasons, a not-so-well-off person living in a rich country may be at a great disadvantage even though her absolute income is significantly higher than the average for the rest of the world.

Thus, in order to characterize poverty, one must take into consideration different ways of converting income into capabilities. Here the relevant concept is "*inadequacy* (for generating minimally acceptable capabilities), rather than absolute *lowness* (independently of the circumstances that influence the conversion)".[64]

We have seen how, for Sen, freedom is the possibility a person has to obtain what he or she chooses, and equality is the opportunity he or she has to develop the maximum number of capabilities, these being understood as what a person may have and may be. As against other concepts, it is important to stress that the idea of capability is sensitive to personal and cultural variety. What a social policy must value are the elements that permit development of capabilities, which go from the most basic to the most complex.

Finally, on proposing the development of capabilities Sen is in agreement with an idea of Rawls, *viz.* that self-respect is "perhaps the most important primary good"; a theory of justice as fairness must therefore make it the center of its attention. Thus institutional arrangements and public policies must exercise influence so that the "social bases of self-respect" may be achieved.[65] For Sen, in the final instance, self-respect is self-esteem and this reflects an adequate development of capabilities.

---

[64] Ibid., pp. 211–213.
[65] A. Sen, "The Political Economy of Targeting", p. 13.

In spite of the impact that Sen's work has had on the study of the criteria of distribution in countries with a high index of poverty, two problems have been noted. Bernard Williams, for example, finds a difficulty in the way we have of measuring capabilities. He believes that a trivialization may take place if we allow commodities to be seen as a basis for generating capabilities. Such an outlook might lead us to suppose that every time we multiply commodities, we multiply capabilities; following this approach, any increase in commodities available would create new capabilities, out of pure logical necessity.[66]

Another problem, mentioned by some economists, is that a distribution linked to capabilities generates a new series of measurement problems. This is due to the fact that individuals' capabilities are rarely observed as such; what is observed is, rather, their achievements. The relation between capabilities and achievements is, however, not straightforward or direct, but depends on the preferences of individuals to attain them.[67]

NEEDS AND PREFERENCES

Some authors concerned with distributive justice have suggested the desirability of a mixed principle, in other words, they do not only consider preferences but also recognize that the range of possibilities before which a person exercises a choice is often beyond her control. G.A. Cohen, like Dworkin, observes that some inequalities are due to the exercise of peoples' preferences, while others that are alien to them. Thus it is necessary to stipulate a principle that takes into account the satisfaction of basic needs when such satisfaction does not belong to a range of choice. To the degree that needs are satisfied we approach a lesser inequality of "access to advantage" made possible by the exercise of preferences.[68] In this case we understand by access both the opportunity to have a preference and the capacity to execute it.

---

[66] See Bernard Williams, "The Standard of Living: Interests and Capabilities", pp. 94 ff.

[67] See E. Skoufias, B. David, and J. Behrman, "Evaluación del sistema de selección de familias beneficiarias en PROGRESA", p. 84.

[68] See G.A. Cohen, "On the Currency of Egalitarian Justice", p. 916, and "Equality of What?", p. 28.

An author who shares this previous idea is Le Grand. He suggests that:

> our judgments as to the degree of inequity inherent in a given situation depends on the degree to which we see that situation as the outcome of individual choice. If one individual receives less than another due to his own choice, then the disparity is not considered inequitable; if it arises for reasons beyond his control, then it is inequitable. This idea can be expressed more formally as follows. Define the factors beyond a person's control as his constraints. These constraints limit the range of possibilities over which an individual can make his choices. Define the set of possibilities bounded by the individual's constraints as his choice set. Then a situation is equitable if it is the outcome of individuals choosing over equal choice sets.[69]

This conception has the advantage not only of incorporating judgments on the inequality that exists in the groups of choice but also of including the idea that injustices derive not only from agents' choices and preferences but also from factors that are beyond their control. If that which is beyond the control of individuals has to do with the lack of a good, without which they would suffer harm, then we are in the presence of a basic need. To the degree that the satisfaction of needs is attended to, the possibility of exercising preferences in increased. Obviously when we speak of individuals who are in a situation of extreme poverty we must recognize that their group of choice is very limited; nonetheless, it is important that the exercise of a preference becomes a habit or a practice. According to this proposal the blank space of the phrase that has to serve as a "pattern" for distribution will be filled in as follows: "To each according to his needs, so that he may exercise his preferences".

In the rest of this chapter I shall examine the way in which a program for combating extreme poverty, PROGRESA, tries to apply the criteria for distribution.

PROGRESA AND THE CRITERIA FOR DISTRIBUTION

The document the principles of this program were set forth states that:

> PROGRESA seeks to remove obstacles preventing poor families having access to sufficient levels of nutrition and health care, as well as benefiting from the train-

---

[69] Julian Le Grand, "Equity as an Economic Objective", pp. 190–191.

ing and development of the *capabilities* that an adequate basic education provides. PROGRESA seeks, essentially, to ensure that such families, who live in contexts of high marginalization, should have access to genuine opportunities for
satisfying their *basic needs* as represented by education, health and food for the
development of their members and for family well-being.[70]

Further on we find that:

> The monetary support provided by PROGRESA is aimed at supplementing fami-
> lies' incomes and improving their levels of consumption, as well as making it
> possible for families to *decide* the best way of exercising this additional purchase
> power.[71]

For this reason we have analyzed the concepts of needs, capabilities, and—as a consequence of decision—preferences.

PROGRESA is a program aimed at satisfying basic needs and making available the minimum means for individuals to exercise their
autonomy or their preferences. The following seeks to explain how
the types of support—both in kind and in cash—function.

Educational support is aimed at supporting enrollment and continuing school attendance of the children of families selected for
assistance, and ensuring their full benefit from attendance. The educational component takes the form of grants and the provision of
books and other equipment. Thus according to the Guidelines:

> Educational grants are assigned to each child or young person under eighteen
> from those families benefiting from the Program, enrolled and attending school
> [...] from the third grade of primary school to the third grade of secondary in
> primary and secondary schools in the normal school attendance regime. The
> grants are awarded during the months of the academic year. Furthermore, at sec-
> ondary level, grants for girls are slightly higher than those for boys, in order to
> stimulate a higher level of attendance by girls at school. This is in response to
> evidence that in families suffering extreme poverty it is the girls who tend—in a
> greater proportion and earlier on than boys—to abandon their studies.[72]

Moreover, children enrolled at school receive monetary support at
the beginning of each year to buy school equipment. The support
provided by PROGRESA in the first semester of 1999 was as follows

---

[70] CONPROGRESA, *Lineamientos generales para la operación del Program de Educación, Salud y Alimentación*, p. 5 (my italics).
[71] Ibid., p. 50.
[72] Ibid., p. 31.

(in Mexican pesos). Food support: $115.00. Educational Component: Grants, *Primary*, third grade $75.00; fourth $90.00, fifth $115.00; sixth $150.00. *Community courses*, level II $75.00; level III $120.00. *Secondary*, first: boys $220.00, girls $235.00; second: boys $235.00, girls $260.00; third: boys $245.00, girls $285.00. Maximum monetary support: $695.00. Maximum educational grant: $580.00. Equipment support: primary: $135.00, secondary: $170.00.

With regard to health, PROGRESA tries to satisfy basic needs through measures of attention to health and various ways of preventing and attending to malnutrition. Thus,

> Attention to health is provided via the application of the Health Services Basic Package, consisting of thirteen types of action characterized by their high degree of effectiveness and their mainly preventive nature, without overlooking action to curing and controlling the principal illnesses. From the point of view of its impact on the general state of the population's health, the most important thing is to apply an orientation anticipating the potential occurrence of diseases.[73]

---

[73] The actions included in the Health Services Basic Package are as follows: 1) basic health measures at the family level which includes actions such as control of harmful fauna, disinfecting of water at the domestic level; sanitary disposal of rubbish; 2) family planning in the form of guidance and provision of contraceptive methods, identification of the population at risk, information for the application of the IDU, tubal ligation, vasectomy, treatment of infertility, education and promotion of reproductive health; 3) prenatal attention, and attention to birth and puerperium, and of the newborn, which implies identification of pregnant women, prenatal consultation, application of tetanus toxoids, administering iron and folic acid, identifying women with high-risk pregnancies, attention to birth and immediate care of newborn, application of SABIN and BCG vaccines to the new-born, attention during puerperium, promotion of maternal lactation; 4) attention to nutrition and infant growth including identification of children under five, diagnosis, follow-ups on undernourished children, diagnosis of nutritional state, nutritional guidance, referral and counter-referral, guidance of mothers, administration of micronutrients; 5) immunization, in the form of administration of vaccines in accordance with the guidelines of the National Vaccination Handbook; 6) treatment of diarrhea cases in the home as part of the training and guidance of mothers, treatment of cases, distribution and use of physiological saline solutions, health education, referral of complicated cases; 7) anti-parasitic treatment of families involving the periodic administration of anti-parasitic drugs to close family members; 8) treatment of acute respiratory infections including training of mothers, referral for treatment, specific treatment; 9) prevention and control of pulmonary tuberculosis involving identification of people with a cough, primary treatment, studies of contacts and measures of protection, reinforced treatment; 10) prevention and control of arterial hypertension and

The prevention of, and attention to, malnutrition is one of the most important elements for the distribution of health, since,

> As Hafdan Mahler, former director-general of the World Health Organization, once put it: "Everywhere it appears that health workers consider that the 'best' health care is one where everything known to medicine is applied to every individual,, by the highest trained medical scientist, in the most specialized institution". As against this medicalization of health care, WHO's 'Health For All' strategy has emphasized the interdependence between health and socio-economic development and the importance of primary care: that is, people's awareness of and response to their own health problems and a recognition that health care is dependent upon housing, water purity and supply, transport, mass media, communications and so on...[74]

a vision, in other words, which goes beyond the medical consideration of illnesses to take in the whole field of social justice.

Prevention, according to the PROGRESA guidelines, consists not only in such measures as vaccinations in accordance with the National Vaccination Handbook; it also embraces attention to nutrition and the food supplements allocated to children aged between four months and two years, to children aged from two to four who present some degree of malnutrition, and to pregnant women and lactating mothers. These supplements supply 100 per cent of daily requirements of micronutrients and 20 per cent of calorie needs.

Finally, it is important to stress that PROGRESA provides a food component via direct monetary support to enable families to improve the quantity and quality of their food consumption, and thus raise their nutritional level. The support is provided in the form of a single monthly payment per family, irrespective of their place of residence,

---

diabetes mellitus involving detection, diagnosis and treatment of cases of arterial hypertension and diabetes mellitus, control of cases; 11) prevention of accidents and initial handling of lesions consisting in provision of first aid in cases of injuries, burns, dislocations, exposed fractures, poisonings, referral of cases, education and promotion for health, including prevention of accidents; 12) community training in self-care including health promotion, protection of sources of food provision for self-consumption, care of the health in general and use of services; 13) prevention and detection of cervico-uterine cancer, involving health promotion for groups at risk, early detection through the study of cervical cytology, oriented towards the early identification of alterations in the cells of the neck of the uterus and early treatment when studies are positive. All actions are accompanied by a health education program.

[74] Cited by: Max Charlesworth, *Bioethics in a Liberal Society*, pp. 117–118.

size or composition. On the other hand, economic support stimulates family members, especially women, to develop their own personal autonomy.

This support aims to foster the responsibility of parents as regards their children's education, health and nutrition and, at the same time, to promote a responsible attitude on the part of families so that resources also benefit the community. The possibility of using economic support in the best way possible fosters a sense of responsibility in individuals for the decisions they make and their consequences.

Nonetheless, certain problems have arisen in practice. The first involves difficulties regarding the provision of the educational and medical services. With the implementation of PROGRESA, school enrollment and visits to the medical services have grown considerably. In some communities it has been observed that medical and educational services and their infrastructure are insufficient to meet the increased demand or to comply with the specific objectives of the program; hence the necessity for communities themselves to learn to watch over both the functioning of the infrastructure and the conduct of school teachers and those who man the health centers. It is thus necessary to perfect the mechanisms so that demands are attended to adequately.

Another matter worth taking into account is that of the heterogeneity of cultures that exists in Mexico. Authors who defend multiculturalism have highlighted the importance of taking these cultural differences into consideration. Thus Michael Walzer has stated that public policies must take seriously three ideals: first, that the state should defend not only individual rights but also collective ones; second, that it should foster the historic celebrations of the different identities; third, that the taxation system should be made fairer and more efficient so that ethnic communities can be provided with more financial help for bilingual educational programs and welfare services with a group orientation.[75] Part of the debate that has taken place in Mexico concerning PROGRESA has involved cultural differences and the particularities of the communities, as against the basic needs approach, which lays down the amount of economic support to be given in all localities, irrespective of geographical and cultural differences. The opinion of the present writer is that, while cultural

---

[75] See Michael Walzer, "Pluralism: A Political Perspective", p. 149.

environments—which may vary as regards different ways of satisfying needs—ought to be taken into consideration, the needs as such must be seen as invariable. As some of the philosophers referred to above have pointed out, these cannot be deprived of their universal nature. It is only after satisfying them that human beings can become truly human.

One aspect of distribution that we have not taken into consideration in this chapter is the matter of constitutional rights: the right to education and health, for example. In view of the central importance of such social rights and the richness of the discussion to which they have given rise, I have devoted a separate chapter to this question.

III

THE RIGHTS OF THE POOR AND OUR OBLIGATIONS
TOWARD THEM

> A man went down from Jerusalem to Jericho, and
> fell among thieves, which stripped him of his
> raiment, and wounded him, and departed, leaving
> him half dead. And by chance there came down a
> certain priest that way: and when he saw him, he
> passed by on the other side. And likewise a
> Levite [...] came and looked on him, and passed
> by on the other side. But a certain Samaritan, as
> he journeyed, came where he was: and when he
> saw him he had compassion on him. And went to
> him, and bound up his wounds, pouring in oil and
> wine, and set him on his own beast, and brought
> him to an inn, and took care of him. And on the
> morrow when he departed, he took out two
> pence, and gave them to the host, and said unto
> him. Take care of him, and whatsoever thou
> spendest more, when I come again, I will repay
> thee. Which now of these three, thinkest thou,
> was neighbour unto him that fell among the
> thieves? And he said, He that showed mercy on
> him. Then said Jesus unto him, Go, and do thou
> likewise.
>
> Luke, 10: 30–37 (Authorized Version).

INTRODUCTION

When we think about the subject of poverty we can hardly avoid
thinking also in terms of certain claims that every citizen has, along
with the constitutional right to demand the satisfaction of such
claims; but it is difficult to think of rights without also taking into
consideration obligations, which are the counterpart of rights. This
chapter therefore addresses to subject of rights and obligations in
connection with poverty. One way of approaching the question of the
criteria of distribution starts off from the notion of "rights"; some
basic needs, as for example health and education, are stipulated as
such in many national constitutions. The thesis of distribution on the

basis of rights has the advantage that individuals may demand fulfillment of such rights. My own country is no exception; with regard to education, for example, an official document issued by the Mexican Government states the following: "In Mexico, the Constitution establishes the right to education. Until 1992, obligatory basic education was limited to the six years of primary schooling. Later, basic education was extended by a further three years in order to include secondary education."[1]

The enshrinement of a right commits us to respecting the demand for its fulfillment; once it is affirmed that all citizens have the right both to health and education, they may demand the conditions to exercise these rights, and the State has the obligation to grant them. Nonetheless, this position presents serious problems. One of these has to do specifically with the concept of a right in itself, and the other with the putting into practice of social rights. This discussion has taken place, in political philosophy, between the proponents of the minimal "night-watchman" state and those of the welfare state.

This chapter addresses the problem of rights and obligations in order to try to apply it to the problem of poverty. For this purpose I shall refer to approaches that deal with the moral correlation between rights and obligations, i.e. which hold that we can only assign rights to those who generate obligations, and that obligations of necessity correspond to rights; we shall also examine those theses that uphold the existence of rights without corresponding obligations, as well as those that affirm the existence of obligations without corresponding rights.

In general, it is possible to distinguish three positions on the relation between rights and obligations. First of all, there are thinkers who affirm that only the right to freedom is universal, and thus non-interference in the acts of individuals—as long as such acts do not harm others—is the only corresponding obligation.

On the other hand, there are thinkers who defend the idea of rights to well-being (welfare rights) and incorporate certain basic needs in a schema of such rights. Thus, a theory of rights embraces the establishment of such rights as those to life, liberty of expression, association, etc. But at the same time the theory needs to incorporate those rights that logically imply the action of certain institutions or per-

---

[1] SEDESOL (Ministry of Social Development), *Mexico's New Social Policy*, p. 32.

sons, such as the right to health, food, housing, etc. Thinkers who uphold such theories also defend the right to non-interference and those rights that enable development of personal autonomy.

There are also thinkers who acknowledge the difficulties presented by some theses that defend welfare rights, namely the lack of fit between rights and obligations. They do in fact stress a practical, empirical problem; there is an asymmetrical relation between people's basic needs and the possibility of demanding respect of rights. It is practically impossible for the poor to have access to the relevant legal authorities in order to demand realization of their rights. The defenders of this position maintain that the language of rights, in the case of poverty, is insufficient to account for the satisfaction of certain basic needs and that, therefore, we must accept the use of a language which addresses obligations while leaving aside the question of their arising from corresponding rights.

THE IDEA OF RIGHTS

Joel Feinberg is perhaps one of the philosophers who has had most influence in the defining and distinguishing of the concept of "right". According to Feinberg, a right is "something" that may be pleaded for or demanded against other persons or against the State. An important distinction is that established between rights and liberties. A liberty (or privilege) is simply the absence of a duty. The distinction seems pertinent since it is necessary to distinguish the notion of positive right, for example when I can demand that someone pays me what he owes me, from the concept of positive liberty, such as was put forward by Isaiah Berlin, and which I mentioned in the previous chapter. Seen thus, not all liberties constitute rights, but all rights generate liberties, since "rights contain liberties as components".[2] When we speak of a right we imply that its possessor may claim it by having recourse to authority if necessary.[3] This is not a gift or a favor which arises from an act of love or friendship, and its fulfillment should not generate a sense of gratitude. If, on the other hand, a right is not respected, we can expect a reaction of indignation. A world with such "legal claim-rights" is one in which individuals, as present or future bearers, respect each other and are respected by each other.

[2] See Joel Feinberg, *Social Philosophy*, p. 58.
[3] Ibid. pp. 56–58.

The force of rights cannot be replaced by "benevolence and devotion to duty",[4] by love or compassion, by religious motivations or hierarchical structure.

Feinberg makes a distinction between several classes of rights; all of them, however, are characterized by implying a corresponding duty to act (or to refrain from acting) on the part of someone else.[5] For instance, a person's positive right is one that corresponds to a positive act performed by others; a negative right is that which somebody has to another's abstaining from some action. If one person has a positive right, someone else has the duty to do something; in the case of a negative right, someone else has the duty to refrain from doing something. Negative rights are those which protect a person against the interference of others.

On the other hand, when we discuss welfare rights, another problem arises concerning the relation between rights and duties; "it is often said that there can be no rights without duties, and that a prior condition for the acquisition or possession of rights is the ability and willingness to shoulder duties and responsibilities", says Feinberg.[6] If we accept this thesis, we shall have to defend the moral correlation between rights and duties, which consists in the acceptation of obligations as a price to be paid for the possession of rights. The thesis of moral correlation is quite different from the logical correlation between rights and duties mentioned above: the idea that any attribution of rights to one person implies the existence of at least one other persons who has a duty towards the former.

The thesis of moral correlation seems a "plausible account of most legal rights [since these] are conferred by general rules that apply to classes of persons rather than to individuals". Generally, individuals tend to belong both to the class to which they the rights in question are adjudicated, and to that upon which the obligations are imposed; thus most laws apply to all citizens without distinction. As Feinberg goes on to observe,

> That version of the moral correlativity doctrine that makes a man's rights conditional upon his exercise of corresponding duties to others is neither logically nec-

---

[4] Ibid., p. 58.
[5] Ibid., p. 59.
[6] Ibid., p. 61.

essary nor morally desirable in every case. But there is no doubt that in many cases it is morally plausible.[7]

The doctrine of logical correlativity, on the other hand, upholds that the rights of one person are necessarily linked to the duties of another. If we take this to mean that *all* rights imply duties on the part of others, and that *all* duties imply other peoples' rights, we shall readily see that in the legal field this doctrine is open to doubt. There are, in fact, duties that are not related to the rights of others; such as the obligations to obey the transit regulations, for instance. Charitable duties are another example. According to Feinberg this is simply due to our customary use of the word *duty* to designate "*any* action understood to be *required*"; in this customary usage, "'duty' tends to be used for any action we feel we *must* (for whatever reason) do".[8]

If, on the other hand, we do accept the thesis of logical correlativity between rights and duties, as long as we defend somebody's right we are implying that someone else has a duty. Since what interests us here is the specific question of welfare rights, it is useful to make a distinction between the words "right" and "claim", since this clarifies the problem associated with logical correlativity. The defenders of the logical correlation thesis would hold that certain rights, as for instance that to education, are, more properly, "claims". When we use the word right in the sense of a "claim" we are referring to a need or a demand that is not necessarily directed at any one person in particular.[9]

Feinberg notes that a considerable number of thinkers have defended the connection that exists between the fact of making a claim and having a right. Some identify right and claim without any kind of qualification; others define a right as a "justified and justifiable claim, or recognized claim, or valid claim"[10]. Feinberg holds that "Having a claim to X is not (yet) the same as having a right to X", but is, rather, to be understood as *"having a case*, consisting of relevant reasons of at least minimal plausibility, that one has a right to X. The case establishes a right, not to X, but to a fair hearing and considera-

---

[7] Ibid., p. 62.
[8] Ibid., p. 63.
[9] Ibid., p. 64.
[10] Ibid., p. 65.

tion. Claims, so conceived, differ in degree; some are stronger than others".[11] Thus, if we understand education as a claim, the reasons for supporting primary education may well make it a stronger claim than that for subsidizing higher education. "Rights, on the other hand, do not differ in degree; no one right is more of a right than another".[12] The widespread use of the word "right" has led to some welfare claims being regarded as positive rights, although, as we have already seen, these, in the strict sense, imply a demand that someone else is under the obligation to meet.

Another reason why we ought to avoid identifying rights with claims is the way in which these words are used in international law and in politics. In politics the word "claim" is often used in reference to the basic needs of human beings in a situation of scarcity. Poor people "everywhere in the world *need* good upbringings, balanced diets, education…", etc.; nevertheless, in many countries, given the scarcity of resources, it is impossible to satisfy these needs. In truth, there is "a moral principle that *all* basic human needs ought to be recognized as "claims". Feinberg accepts that "natural needs are real claims" that merit attention and serious consideration, but which cannot be treated as rights that impose obligations.[13]

Feinberg's position leads us to the conclusion that only those rights that impose obligations may be regarded as "rights" in the strict sense. Welfare rights are not always conducive to the assignment of obligations, and when, for example, the state is the agent charged with the duty, it is not always in a position to comply with the corresponding right. One should, however, emphasize the important role of such rights in political discussion as claims that must be attended to or at least taken seriously. As Mark Platts—referring to certain articles of the Universal Declaration of Human Rights of 1948 that set forth rights such as the right to work, to periodic paid vacations, to food, clothing, housing and medical attention— observes:

> I do not doubt the high desirability of the contents of these supposed rights; neither do I doubt that a world where all enjoyed such things would be much more civilized than the world that actually exists […] What I *do* doubt is that this use

---

[11] Ibid., p. 66.
[12] Loc. cit.
[13] Ibid., pp. 66–67.

of the vocabulary of *human rights* is compatible with that which aims at capturing the distinctive nature of the concept of law—and what is distinctively important about this concept. The abuse of the said concept tends to be highly dangerous, and not only from an intellectual point of view.[14]

It is important to point out that both Platts and Feinberg are in agreement on the desirability of such "rights" as aims to be fought for in the political arena.

DEFENSE OF RIGHTS IN THE "STRICT SENSE"

While Feinberg admits that in the political field demands may make themselves felt as claims for which reasons can be offered that justify their being seen as rights, there are other authors who deny such a thesis. These writers hold that the only defendable rights are those that entail assignable obligations; welfare rights do not, and thus give rise to conflicts in our legal systems.

Criticism of welfare rights rests on three theses: one moral, one political and one economic. The moral criticism is based on the idea that individuals have certain rights that may only in justice be limited if their exercise endangers the rights of others; only in such circumstances is the State obliged to intervene. Otherwise, nobody has the right to prevent us from attaining our proposed goals since we are moral persons endowed with autonomy and dignity; nobody is entitled to make us do something we do not wish to do. We are to be treated as ends and not only as means. Welfare rights lead to our goals and purposes being altered, because the State can obligate us to carry out certain actions in order that others may attain their goals. The political thesis, on the other hand, refers to the State's obligation to protect us and to avoid certain preferences being imposed upon us. A State that imposes duties on certain persons in order to satisfy the welfare rights of other members of the community is a paternalist State which expands its attributions in an illegitimate way since it treats individuals as if they were incapable of deciding for themselves.

One of the defenders of the minimal State is Robert Nozick who believes that any distributive principle violates the liberty of individuals. The only principle worthy of being taken into account is that

---

[14] Mark Platts, *Sobre usos y abusos de la moral*, p. 97.

which states that distribution must be effected "From each as they choose, and to each as they are chosen".[15]

Finally, the economic thesis refers to the burden imposed by welfare rights upon taxpayers. This has resulted in considerable inefficiency in services, has created perverse incentives and has had harmful effects both on taxpayers and beneficiaries.

One criticism of welfare rights derives from the idea of the logical correlation between duties and obligations. For example, the rights to exercise certain liberties have sense because such rights imply the obligation of others to respect them. On the contrary, welfare rights impose obligations upon persons who did not previously accept them and which, therefore, do not depend upon voluntary actions. A thinker who attacks the idea of welfare rights offers the following example:

> I am obliged not to murder or steal from other individuals, even those I have never encountered and with whom I have no relationship. But am I obliged to respect their welfare rights? No advocate of welfare rights would say that a poor person has a right to appear at my door and demand food, or a place to sleep, or any of the other goods to which he is said to have a right. The obligation to supply those goods does not fall upon me as a particular individual; it falls upon us all indifferently, as members of society [...] Insofar as welfare rights are implemented through government programs, for example, the obligation is distributed among all taxpayers.[16]

David Kelly, like Nozick, thinks that welfare rights simply have no validity: there are no arguments that can defend them. Rights such as education, health, housing, have been implemented by obliging people to pay taxes. In this way the State has made of charity an obligatory matter; consequently, acts of genuine benevolence aimed at helping those persons who find themselves in a situation of extreme poverty disappear. The only efficient mechanism for promoting the well-being of a community is the market, which is also the only system that respects the rights of individuals and their voluntary actions; private savings plans, for example, would cater better for people's retirement needs than obligatory state pension schemes. There is simply no need to supplant the market as guarantor of the

---

[15] R. Nozick, *Anarchy, State, and Utopia*, p. 160.
[16] David Kelley, *A Life of One's Own*, p. 24.

basic satisfiers through the implementation of government pro-grams.[17]

As we may observe, rights in the strict sense are manifestations of a kind of simple legal relation in which individuals know perfectly what their reciprocal rights and duties are; welfare rights, on the other hand, require a previous framework of organizational norms lacking immediate enforceability. This in turn generates a multiplic-ity of legal obligations on the part of different subjects, whose joint fulfillment is necessary for the full satisfaction of the right.[18]

To conclude this section, we must point out that one reason for criticizing welfare rights is the impossibility, in most situations, of the State's actually satisfying them. Another reason is the fiscal bur-den and thus the limitation on freedom that some citizens have to bear and which makes it difficult for them to carry out their life plans. A third source of criticism lies in the need for the State to cre-ate inefficient bureaucratic apparatuses incapable of generating the benefits which would be attained if the free play of the market was allowed to function without interference. Perhaps one of the most forthright expressions of the notion of the undesirability of social rights was expressed by Rhodes Boyson in an article entitled "Fare-well to Paternalism", where he stated the following:

> The moral fiber of our people has been weakened. A state which does for its citi-zens what they can do for themselves is an evil state; and a state which removes all choice and responsibility from its people and makes them like broiler hens will create the irresponsible society. In such an irresponsible society, no one ca-res, no one saves, no one bothers—why should they when the state spends all its energies taking money from the energetic, successful and thrifty to give it to the idle, the failures and the feckless.[19]

DEFENSE OF WELFARE RIGHTS

It is important to stress that none of the authors who "take rights seriously" deny the value of rights "in the strict sense". They believe such rights to be necessary, but insufficient, to enable people to fur-ther their life plans.

---

[17] Ibid., p. 151.

[18] See Luis Prieto Sanchís, "Los derechos sociales y el principio de igualdad", p. 25.

[19] Cited by Anthony Skillen, "Welfare State versus Welfare Society?", p. 203.

Carlos Nino,[20] points to certain contradictions in the thinking of those who defend rights "in the strict sense", (whom he refers to as "conservative liberals"). One of these lies in the supposition that the market is a "spontaneous order" that generates equitable mechanisms of distribution. For Nino, nothing could be further from the truth since the market is based on a structure of property which is established by means of deliberately promulgated and applied statutory laws; these laws ratify certain acts of possession and transference of goods which might not otherwise be recognized, attributing to them certain rights and obligations—of varying scope—while laying down punitive sanctions against those who interfere with them. Such laws are applied by courts of law and police forces maintained out of income derived from the obligations of taxpayers.[21]

For Nino, the second confusion affecting conservative liberalism consists in its conception of personal autonomy as "constituted by negative conditions, such as the non-interference of third parties" without taking into account its need for "goods and resources that must be provided not only through non-interference but also by the active behavior of third parties", in order for certain sections of the population to be in a position to choose and realize their life plans. Defenders of liberal rights uniformly deny that rights can be violated by omission.[22]

Judgment regarding political "acts" by omission is a complicated philosophical problem—among other things because of the difficulty of determining when a series of events is due to an action or an omission, the difficulty of establishing a difference between the point of view of the agent and that of the moral critic, and the impossibility of our feeling responsible for all our omissions.[23] Nonetheless, Philippa Foot[24] makes an important distinction in arguing that the rights of individuals may be affected when certain persons or institutions fail to do something. Having made an initial distinction between allowing and causing, she then differentiates two senses of allowing. First of all, there is "the allowing which is forbearing to prevent": there is a train of events already in march and there is

---

[20] C.S. Nino, "Sobre los derechos sociales", p. 138.

[21] Ibid.

[22] Ibid. pp. 138–139.

[23] See Jonathan Glover, *Causing Death and Saving Lives*, chap. 7.

[24] Philippa Foot, "The Problem of Abortion", pp. 25–26.

something that someone could do in order to prevent it. In the second sense, to allow refers to the idea of *enabling* something to happen: removing an obstacle that is preventing a train of events from unfolding. Foot relates the difference between causing something and allowing it (in the first sense) with the distinction between negative and positive duties. The former refer to the obligation to abstain from doing something (for example, desisting from hurting someone), and the latter to the obligation to do something (for example, to help another).[25] The defenders of welfare rights argue that an infringement of the autonomy of the individual takes place when a train of events is underway—the existence of starvation or malnutrition for instance—and nothing is done to prevent it.

Finally, the third confusion of the defenders of rights "in the strict sense" lies in the culpability assigned to the State when it obliges certain members of society to pay taxes which are then destined to others. Nino thinks that those who have the duty to guarantee welfare rights are:

> All the citizens in a broad sense—*in a general conjunctive way*—to use the terminology of G. H. von Wright. It is they who are under the obligation to carry out actions like paying taxes, so that citizens whose autonomy is diminished may have resources that enable them to enjoy a similar autonomy to the rest.[26]

However, in spite of the defense of welfare rights the doubt arises concerning the kind of obligations these impose on us. We need an analysis of those obligations whose non- fulfillment is not subject to coercion by the State, in other words, those that refer to the duty of the more fortunate citizens to respond to the welfare rights of the rest. Due to the difficulties that arise when we speak of welfare rights, some philosophers, as I have already mentioned, regard it as necessary to lay the emphasis on duties. While putting the emphasis on duties may well lessen the force of rights as claims; these may still be our trump cards when we seek to establish agreements and responsibilities with those who find themselves in a situation of poverty.

---

[25] Ibid., p. 27–28.
[26] Carlos Nino, op. cit., p. 142.

THE IDEA OF DUTIES

As we saw at the beginning of this chapter, the satisfaction of certain basic needs is situated at the center of the debate on rights; yet the concept of duty is also intimately connected with it. There is no doubt at all that a source of such a duty lies in the absence of those elements that satisfy the basic needs of some citizens. Thus, as James Griffin remarks,[27] the attraction of the explanation of obligations on the basis of needs comes from our deep intuition of its great moral significance. He thinks, however, that such explanations as we have dealt with above, are over-rigid and may only with difficulty work as a basis for establishing duties. According to Griffin, the more easily a need can be satisfied, the least important it is, since once it is satisfied it disappears.[28] we may recognize the importance of a need by the level of satisfaction of other basic needs. Griffin tells us:

> ...if my needs for liberty and minimum material provision are not met, and are so unlikely ever to be met that life is not worth living, then health must matter less too. And if the amount to which a basic need will be met is only slightly affected by some change, we can regard the change as of little importance. We can then amend the need account of well-being: *well-being is the level to which basic needs are met so long as they retain importance.*[29]

Basic needs can be a source of obligations since they involve the satisfaction of certain goods that we regard as essential, simply because we are human beings. Such goods are necessary and sufficient for recognizing that an existence is human. The perception of the non-satisfaction of basic needs in one part of the population, ought to give rise to the obligation to establish certain conditions for them to be satisfied in the other. If we could manage to identify a motivation that justifies the obligation to help, we would have more arguments available to us in defense of welfare rights.

We shall now go on to examine two arguments that enable us to justify the obligation we have towards people in a situation of extreme poverty. The first of these is based on a "consequentialist" form of ethics, originating in the thought of Mill; the second is an ethics of principles of clearly Kantian extraction.

---

[27] James Griffin, *Well-Being*, p. 45.

[28] Ibid., p. 51.

[29] Ibid., p. 52.

OBLIGATIONS FROM THE POINT OF VIEW OF CONSEQUENCES

Peter Singer,[30] addressing the problem of poverty, has set forward a principle for justifying what we might call the "duty to assist". This principle states that "if it is in our power to prevent something very bad from happening, without thereby sacrificing anything of comparable moral significance, we ought to do it".

According to Singer, if we take the principle seriously, our lives and the world in which we live will be substantially better, since we would apply this to people who live in extreme poverty. Singer tells us: "Helping is not, as conventionally thought, a charitable act which is praiseworthy to do, but not wrong to omit; it is something that everyone ought to do".[31]

Singer offers an argument in favor of the obligation to provide assistance:

> First premise: If we can prevent something bad without sacrificing anything of comparable significance, we ought to do it.
>
> Second premise: Absolute poverty is bad.
>
> Third premise: There is some absolute poverty we can prevent without sacrificing anything of comparable moral significance.
>
> Conclusion: We ought to prevent some absolute poverty.[32]

According to Singer, the first premise—upon which the argument hangs—is the substantive moral premise. The second can only with difficulty be rejected, since absolute poverty lies beyond the limits of what could possibly be described as human decency; it is impossible to encounter an ethical position that does not regard it as a bad thing and one which deserves to be combated. The third expresses the idea that absolute poverty can be avoided without sacrificing anything of comparable moral significance. This premise avoids the objection that any help offered to the poor is only a drop in the ocean and does not help significantly to reduce poverty in the world. According to Singer, he answer to the objection is found in the thesis that any situation of absolute poverty is bad, and not only the total quantity. If we do not sacrifice anything that has a comparable moral signifi-

---

[30] Peter Singer, *Practical Ethics*, p. 229.

[31] Ibid., p. 230.

[32] Ibid., p. 230.

cance we may yet help just one family or one person and, if we accept this, we justify the third premise.[33]

Singer compares his position with that of Robert Nozick, for whom it is quite possible to accumulate wealth without incurring any obligation to share it with someone else. The only requirement contained in Nozick's theory is that individuals acquire their property without engaging in fraudulent or coactive actions; nothing prevents us from enjoying our belongings even when there are people dying of hunger. What Nozick rejects are obligatory measures such as taxes; in place of these, he proposes acts of charity.

To show that this is just a way of thinking, Singer has recourse to the theory of St. Thomas of Aquinas, who thought that while the rich had the right to enjoy their wealth, they, nonetheless, had obligations toward the poor. Socialists, on the other hand, believe that welfare should be seen from the point of view of the community and not from that of individuals. Utilitarians, too, would be willing to abstain from defending property rights if they could thereby avoid a greater harm.[34]

Perhaps the most serious objections offered against the principle, as we saw in Chapter I, are those of neo-Malthusianism and triage. Let us recall that the former refers to the overpopulation that neo-Malthusians believe is generated by policies of fighting poverty, and the latter to the supposedly unproductive drain on limited resources entailed in attending to people who are in a state of extreme poverty.

Singer affirms that we can reject such objections by recourse to a "consequentialist" ethics. This must take into account the probabilities of a number of different consequences occurring. The consequences of neo-Malthusian policies and triage would be undesirable since population would be controlled through the application of hunger and death. In this way we would condemn a large part of the population to live in a state of absolute poverty beyond any humanly acceptable limit.

The provision of assistance to those who are below the extreme poverty line can in fact be justified in the very objections mentioned at the beginning of this section. Governments ought to commit themselves to implementing public policies aimed at the poorest members

---

[33] Ibid., p. 231.
[34] Ibid., p. 234.

of the population; if efforts were stepped up to combat deficiencies in education and nutrition, and to make available birth control methods, this would undoubtedly contribute to controlling demographic growth. The evidence suggests that it is possible to reduce population growth by improving economic security and education, while also promoting birth control campaigns. This kind of project completely overturns any Malthusian objection to the principle of helping the poor.[35]

A final objection to the principle of the duty to help is that it demands a moral level difficult to attain. This objection has been expressed in three different forms. The first of these puts the emphasis on human nature. If human beings are not capable of reaching such moral levels, it makes little sense to demand that they do so; nobody has the right to demand the impossible. This version is upheld by certain evolutionists: i.e. we are how we are because the way we are has proved successful; human relations are by nature partial, and natural altruism extends at the most to making sacrifices for our families and friends—never for people we have not even met. The second version states that even if we were to reach such a high moral standard, it would be undesirable to make our assistance an obligation; this is the position of people like Susan Wolf, who criticizes the notion of human beings as "moral saints"; if we all devoted ourselves to doing good to others, we would distort our existence to the extent of having to neglect much of what makes life not merely bearable but actually worthwhile. The third maintains that it "is undesirable to set so high a standard because it will be perceived as too difficult to reach, and will discourage many from even attempting to do so [...] setting a lower standard might actually result in more aid being given".[36]

Singer affirms—but fails to argue the point—that the principle does not ask too much, that it *is* possible to promote it and to give every encouragement to people concerned for those living in a situation of extreme poverty.

---

[35] Ibid., p. 240.
[36] Ibid., pp. 242–246.

OBLIGATIONS FROM THE POINT OF VIEW OF PRINCIPLES

Onora O'Neill[37] has criticized Singer's consequentialist position; it is her opinion that Singer bases the obligation to attend to the poor on the principle of beneficence; this is basically the principle expressed by Singer that "if it is within our power to prevent something bad from happening, without thereby sacrificing anything of comparable moral importance, we ought morally to do it". As we saw above, Singer rejects the notion of charitable acts—praiseworthy in themselves, but in no way reprehensible if omitted—as a basis for assistance, offering instead the principle (as O'Neill puts it) that "beneficence is a matter of obligation". According to O'Neill, this is a central and substantive ethical affirmation of any consequentialist doctrine. Her criticism of consequentialism is that its defenders view all "obligations [as] fundamentally required because they contribute to human happiness or benefit, and right action is in the first place helpful or beneficent action". Consequentialists defend assistance to others as duties of justice and not of charity; nonetheless, they reduce the duties of justice to "a general duty of beneficence".[38]

O'Neill also criticizes the doctrine based on rights, and does so for three reasons. First, because she accepts the idea that welfare rights lack a correlative obligation and are affected by specific situations such as scarcity and abundance. Like Feinberg, she thinks that the social rights perspective has a very important role as a means of formulating what are valid and justifiable claims, but that these cannot, properly speaking, be considered rights. Secondly, she thinks that the language of rights sets individuals at the level of receivers of benefits; while the movement in favor of human rights has been of great importance, for O'Neill it is a problem that—in the final instance—those who obtain their rights receive "something" from those who have the duty to provide them.[39] Thirdly, she believes that liberal theories based on rights have failed to take into account the virtues as a crucial element in our moral life.[40]

O'Neill proposes a way of explaining our conduct towards people living in a state of extreme poverty by means of the concept of obli-

---

[37] See O. O'Neill, *Faces of Hunger*, p. 57.
[38] Ibid., p. 58.
[39] See Onora O'Neill, *Towards Justice and Virtue*, pp. 134ff.
[40] Ibid., p. 140.

gation. She observes that the language of obligations frequently appears in our daily lives and in our discussions of ethics and politics. She also points out that a possible disadvantage of this kind of language is not so much "that it is unavoidably abstract (and so too indeterminate to guide action), or inaccessible to agents and agencies with the capacities and powers to make changes" as that it "is readily captured by established and establishment categories and assumptions about what problems there are and who ought to do what about them".[41] Thus, if obligations arise as a statutory product of our institutions, of traditions, of our role in society, individuals will always perceive obligations as conservative and guardians of the existing *status quo*.[42]

The implications of this point of view concerning our obligations towards the poor are relatively simple. It is impossible to generate situations that foster changes or that challenge the existing "rules of play". Our duties towards the poor, therefore, will depend on the actions to which our institutions, our traditions, or the role we play in society obligate us.

O'Neill does, nonetheless, believe in the existence of another way of understanding obligations, one that transcends the field of institutions, traditions and social roles. If we can find another way of understanding obligations, we might discover a principle that would enable us to guide our actions correctly. It is important to bear in mind that the way to achieve this does not pass via the theory of recipients—like that held by the defenders of rights—but rather on the agents upon whom the said obligations fall.[43]

O'Neill believes that what we need "is a theory of obligation which is not only *universal and critical* but *accessible to the relevant agents and agencies*". She broaches the problem as follows:

> ...obligations to do or omit actions of various sorts are individuated by act descriptions. We might have obligations to act justly or generously, or more specifically to contribute to grain reserves or to tithe our incomes or not to collect debts from the poor. Obligations are met when those who hold them act and for-

---

[41] O. O'Neill, *Faces of Hunger*, p. 121.

[42] Ibid., p. 122.

[43] O. O'Neill, *Towards Justice and Virtue*, p. 140.

bear in ways specified by certain descriptions. Since descriptions are indeterminate, no obligation wholly specifies the way in which it may be fulfilled.[44]

But while it is true that for the language of obligations to provide us with an explanation and a guide for action, it needs to give us a detailed and accessible description of the actions, it must also provide

> ...more abstract act-descriptions. Even within a determinate social context, where obligations are well specified, transitions from more abstract to more determinate act descriptions are crucial for any process of practical deliberation. [...] Any theory of obligation which can guide action, *even in a local context*, has to provide for moves from more abstract to more specific descriptions of the problems and obligations of particular agents in contexts of action.[45]

It is when we move in the reverse direction that we find ourselves entering into a field of inquiry of a more "open-ended" and ultimately "philosophical" nature:

> There are always many determinate ways of enacting abstractly specified obligations. Some match locally established conceptions of what ought to be done; others do not. The most daily discussions of obligations often dispute whether an action described in specific ways can be seen as falling under other more abstract descriptions.[46]

Another important question for an ethics of obligations concerns the possibility of obtaining a critical overview, of avoiding the mere falling back on traditional practices and institutional roles. To achieve this, a theory of obligation must also include "'neutral' and 'scientific' accounts of problems, policies, and results".[47]

O'Neill states that the principles on which obligations are based do not merely constitute "worthy intentions", but that they may guide our actions and thus our political decisions. But obligations can be "embodied" in various ways, and to appreciate this it is first necessary to distinguish the different categories of obligations. On the one hand, there are the perfect obligations which point towards a relation between the bearers of the obligation and the possessors of the rights.

---

[44] O. O'Neill, *Faces of Hunger*, p. 123.

[45] O. O'Neill, *Toward Justice and Virtue*, p. 147.

[46] Loc. cit.

[47] Ibid., pp. 126–127.

On the other hand, there are the imperfect ones which belong to iden-
tifiable bearers, without the existence of corresponding right-holders.
Cutting across this distinction is another, which classifies obligations
as either *universal* or *special*: while the former can be held by all, the
latter "grow out of specific roles, institutions, relationships or the
like".

Thus perfect obligations include *universal perfect obligations* that
"can be owed to and performed for all others" (these are the "coun-
terparts of liberty rights") and *special perfect obligations* that "are
owed to and performed for specified others"; the former can be "in-
stitutionalized in legal and political systems" that define and uphold
positive rights. The principles of such obligations "can be embodied
in social institutions and in individual characters which reinforce
their primary embodiments. A legal order may gain support from
forms of social solidarity and traditions of fair play". Such forms
must be shared by all those who belong to the above-mentioned social order. On the other hand, special perfect obligations need social
structures or practices which link the bearers of the obligations directly to the possessors of certain rights. "Specific institutions such
as states, markets, firms and families" create and foster special relations for founding such rights and obligations.[48]

Universal imperfect obligations, on the other hand, require their
bearers to perform certain actions, but are not directed toward a pre-
cise recipient. Some obligations of this type "will be most readily
embodied not in relationships between agents and recipients but in
agents' characters, and can be thought of as required virtues of those
agents". Finally, special imperfect obligations, while not requiring
corresponding rights, are nonetheless embodied in the ethos of specific relations and practices of agents, and are often—though not
necessarily—expressed in actions carried out within certain such
relations.[49]

The examples given by O'Neill of each of the obligations are as
follows. Parents believe that they have certain obligations towards
their children. Some of these obligations are due also to all others,
for example not to hurt them. This is a *universal perfect obligation*
since all people have the right not to be hurt. Parents also have the

---

[48] Loc. cit.
[49] See Onora O'Neill, *Toward Justice and Virtue*, pp. 149.

duty to look after and maintain their own children, but not those of others; if they fail to do so, a particular institution may intervene. In this case, we are speaking of a *special perfect obligation*. On the other hand, parents have the obligation to respect and concern themselves both for their own children and for the children of others; this obligation is *universal* and *imperfect*. Finally, good parents have the obligation to treat their children with attention and affection, to provide them with stimuli in life. This is part of the family relationship between parents and children; nonetheless, parents do not have this kind of obligation towards the children of others. An obligation of this sort is both *special* and *imperfect*.[50]

What motivates perfect obligations is the right of others; on the other hand, what motivates fulfillment of imperfect obligations is the existence of virtues.

Now, we may assume that Onora O'Neill's thesis concerning poverty is based on perfect obligations, in the sense of the duties we have towards those who find themselves in a state of powerlessness and vulnerability, and that it would correspond to a universal right to liberty. One universal perfect obligation is that of not exercising coercion against anybody else. While the term "coercion" is problematic, it is doubtless connected to the idea of a threat.[51] For a threat to be credible depends, on the one hand, on the power possessed to inflict harm and, on the other, on the vulnerability to suffer it. One form of vulnerability consists in lacking basic necessities, since people who lack the necessary means to subsistence are dependent upon the exercise of power by those able to provide or deny such means. According to Feinberg, we hurt a man or a woman when we deny them or deprive them of something they need.[52] Thus, to be in a state of basic need reflects a lack of power, and therefore a situation of vulnerability. When a section of the population is vulnerable, it is open to coercion, and such coercion is not necessarily manifested in violent form; it "may well be couched in the language of standard commercial bargaining or political negotiation. [...] Where there are vast differences of power and vulnerability, it is all too easy for the powerful to make the vulnerable 'an offer they cannot refuse'". Ac-

---

[50] Ibid., p. 151.
[51] See O. O'Neill, "Rights, Obligations and Needs", p. 108.
[52] J. Feinberg, op. cit., p. 31.

cording to O'Neil, once we discover the vulnerable aspect of human nature we must take into account what is required for those who have needs not to find themselves in a situation of coercion. One way of making sure that people who find themselves in a situation of extreme poverty are not vulnerable consists in offering them benefits that they can either accept or reject.[53] The idea of justice that she proposes requires changes in the fundamental principles of institutions in order to eliminate the situations that place individuals in such a degree of vulnerability that they lack the capacity to choose or reject what is being offered. The most important change consists in abolishing material needs. To eliminate situations of vulnerability constitutes an obligation, both upon the institutions that implement social policies and upon citizens.

As we have already seen, the obligation not to coerce is both perfect and universal because people have the right not to be coerced. But it is also possible to think that a universal imperfect obligation exists once we incorporate the exercise of virtues. For once we begin to think in terms of obligations rather than rights we are also led to think of the exercise of virtues, and in the case of poverty, principally, that of justice. This perspective sets institutions responsible for satisfying basic needs the task of adopting an active and responsible attitude as opposed to being satisfied with merely assuming, passively, that they complied with the demand of a right. When we accept this general principle, we must learn to let it serve as a guide for performing specific actions.

Once we accept the obligation that we have to help combat poverty not so much on account of the consequences as on principle, we shall have to conclude that any policy must be seen as good from the moral point of view if it coincides with the perfect obligation of making sure that human beings are not coerced.

The theories of obligation mentioned above gave rise to two problems. The first, as I have already mentioned, refers to the importance we may or may not give to the consequences of an action. Motivation based on consequences may affect us if we have a clear vision of such consequences; failing this we would simply feel obliged to help the people closest to us and leave other cases—where we have no perception of the consequences—to fend for themselves. Likewise,

---

[53] O. O'Neill, op. cit. p. 108.

in reference to Singer's consequentialist position, it is not easy to know when we are carrying out an action in which we are not "sacrificing anything of comparable morally significance".

The second problem has its roots in several ethical conceptions. A doubt always arises regarding the pertinent motivation that leads us to consider the obligation and to act upon it. One advantage of consequentialist theories is that a motivation is readily identified in self-interest. Theories of rights, on the other hand, point to a motivation in the concept of autonomy.

An answer is again to be found in O'Neill's work: what motivates us to comply with imperfect obligations is the appearance of certain virtues among which justice is predominant. Let us remember that, for Aristotle,

> The moral virtues are produced in us neither *by* Nature nor *against* nature. Nature, indeed, prepares in us the ground for their reception, but their complete formation is the product of habit. [...] Moral virtues are acquired by first exercising them. [...] We become just by performing just actions...[54]

Now, other attempts have been made to solve the problem of what motivates us to act when we find ourselves in a society which contains individuals whose basic needs are unsatisfied. Christine Korsgaard refers to an argument provided by the philosophy of Kant: "Regarding my needs as normative for others, or, as Kant puts it, making myself an end for others, I must regard the needs of others as normative for me".[55] And to argue in favor of this position, I shall refer to the theses of Thomas Nagel, Luis Villoro and John Rawls.

Nagel[56] accepts that our primary motivation is in accordance with our desire or interest, and that these often constitute a reason for acting. Despite this, he considers that altruistic reasons constitute another motivation for acting. He distinguishes between actions motivated by desires and those that are not. He discusses a thesis that is broadly accepted in philosophy, which holds that while reasons for acting involve a motivational force rooted in desires, there are cases

---

[54] Aristotle, *Nicomachean Ethics*, book II, 1103b (translation adapted from Penguin Classics ed., pp. 55–56).
[55] Christine Korsgaard, *Creating the Kingdom of Ends*, p. 60.
[56] Thomas Nagel, *The Possibility of Altruism*, Princeton, Princeton University Press, 1978.

in which the desire to act is itself generated by reason.[57] The most important cases of desires generated by reason are what we call prudence and altruism, in other words cases in which we are motivated by considerations regarding the future and regarding others. An example of prudence will clarify this idea. It is possible that today there is plenty of food in the house, and I have no desire to go to the shops to buy the food that will be lacking in the future. However, the consideration that in the future I might find myself without anything to eat may give rise to the desire to acquire what I shall later need. There may thus exist a reason that at present lacks a motivational desire but which is capable of generating one on the basis of a situation that can be foreseen in the future.[58]

The same kind of thing happens in the case of altruism; it is possible that certain wishes provide me with a reason to act on behalf of others, as Singer, for instance, holds. Nonetheless, we can act in an altruistic way if we consider that others are people like ourselves with needs, interests and preferences, and that we can put ourselves in their place.[59] The possibility of conceiving a society in which poverty is reduced may motivate us to carry out actions to try to eliminate it. For Nagel, both prudence and altruism rest on objective reasons, in other words they do not depend on the desires of the subjects but on the way in which we perceive certain situations.

In arguing in favor of altruistic reasons Nagel sees the convenience of explaining our actions by taking into account impersonal interests. He insists that an impersonal point of view constitutes the raw material not only of ethics but of any political theory. The idea that underlies what we have termed impersonal interests is the concern that I may feel for others, accompanied by the conviction that others also are concerned about me. These impersonal interests manifest themselves in three stages. First, as a basis, the conviction that the lives of all individuals are equally valuable. Second, the belief in impartiality, in other words in the idea that all individuals are equal. Here we are not speaking of an equality in which each individual counts as an entry of a combinatory function, but of an equality in which a greater weight is given to improving the lives of those

---

[57] Ibid., p. 32.
[58] Ibid., p. 64.
[59] Ibid,. p. 83.

who find themselves in a situation of poverty. The alleviation of the urgent needs of others sets off a motivation to act. Third, it consists in seeing situations "from outside", in other words, as if we were not directly or indirectly involved in them. When we see the world from outside we can realize that the alleviation of poverty and the special consideration for individuals who do not have a minimally acceptable life situation, deserves priority attention.[60] From this perception of the world and the desire to improve it the obligation may arise to help those who lack basic satisfiers.

It is worth mentioning that John Rawls has spoken of certain natural duties that are incumbent upon us irrespective of our voluntary acts. Among these he mentions the natural duty "of helping another when he is in need or jeopardy, provided that one can do so without excessive risk or loss to oneself; the duty not to harm or injure another; and the duty not to cause excessive suffering".[61] Another natural duty mentioned by Rawls has to do with the obligations we have towards the poor, and which consists in "mutual respect". This is the duty to show people the respect due to them as moral persons, in other words, individuals with a sense of justice and a conception of the good. Mutual respect is shown in different ways: through our "willingness to see the situation of others from their point of view, from the perspective of their conception of their good; and in our being prepared to give reasons for our actions whenever the interests of others are materially affected".[62] This way of seeing natural duties agrees with Nagel's thesis of impartiality.

Luis Villoro has also expressed the same idea using the language of values:

> When we think about values it is possible to distinguish two different orders. On the one hand, we have the evaluative qualities experienced in an object or situation; on the other, those attributed to the final states of our actions; these manifest themselves in the projection of possible values. The former are founded on the properties of the world, the latter belong to the imaginary world. But value judgments in both orders must be justified by reasons.[63] The relation of the action to the value is different in one and the other order. We can consider two situations. In a first type of case, the action sets out from the experience of a value or

---

[60] See T. Nagel, *Equality and Partiality*, p. 96.

[61] J. Rawls, *A Theory of Justice*, p. 114.

[62] Ibid., p. 337.

[63] L. Villoro, *El poder y el valor. Fundamentos de una ética política*, p. 31.

a lack. Thus, the perception of given qualities in an object generates a positive attitude towards it, which, in turn—united to certain beliefs—impels us to project the end of an action which satisfies this positive attitude. In other cases, on the other hand, it is the action itself which introduces a new, previously non-existent value. Nothing of the sort was experienced before the action in the world took place. Only a lack was perceived. This lack, together with the belief in the rightness of the situation that might alleviate it, is what impels us to project a valuable end. The action is caused, then, by the positive attitude towards the realization of the imagined end, together with the valuation of this, without there being a previous perception of a value given in the world around us. On the contrary, it is an absence of value that incites us to project the end [...]. The experience of suffering in real society impels us to project in the imagination the ideal order that would alleviate it.[64]

We can thus conclude from Villoro's idea that, once we manage to project the order that would alleviate suffering, we will feel ourselves motivated to carry it out.

And we can conclude with Griffin's idea that basic needs can be a source of obligations because the concept itself implies a claim for certain goods that we consider indispensable simply because we are human beings. Such goods are necessary and sufficient conditions for us to recognize that an existence is human. From the perception of the presence of basic needs in a section of the population, ought then to arise among the rest the obligation to satisfy them. As Paul Spicker, a specialist in studies on poverty, recalls:

The term 'poverty', [...] 'carries with it an implication and moral imperative that something should be done about it. Its definition is a value judgment and should be clearly seen to be so'. To describe people as poor contains the implication that something or other should be done about it.[65]

Now, once we have explained how obligations towards people living in a state of extreme poverty can arise, we may pause to consider on whom such obligations fall. It seems to me that in a democratic political system citizens ought to possess mechanisms enabling them to exercise pressure in order to oblige those in charge of institutions to fulfill their obligations. Of course, the most important organs of pressure should be the legislative and judicial branches of govern-

---

[64] Ibid., p. 32.
[65] In D. Gordon and P. Spicker, *The International Glossary on Poverty*, p. 157 (quoting Piachaud).

ment. As regards the legislative power, in many countries this appears to be at an enormous distance from the needs of those who find themselves in a situation of extreme poverty. Besides, the situation of the poor makes them particularly vulnerable to electoral promises. It naturally happens that the judicial power also grows apart from an important sector of the population. In Mexico an example of this can be found in the *Ley de Amparo* or "writ of *amparo*" law,[66] originally designed to protect constitutional rights against official abuse, concerning which a legislator has recently commented:

> The law has fallen into disrepute due to the technicalities in its drawing up and the requirements laid down for the procedures in its application, with the result that the benefits it offers are now totally out of reach of the ordinary citizen and operate merely to the advantage of those possessing the greatest economic resources.[67]

But also, following Jon Elster, we might think that other mechanisms of pressure exist. Some of these would be the organized groups that promote common goals for all members of society, such as NGOs or other organized interest groups;[68] others might be implemented by public opinion. The latter has an obligation to declare itself on matters that society cannot accept.[69] Nevertheless, when we consider the question of poverty we discover that many NGOs handle the matter as if it were a question of charity rather than justice. As we have already seen, this would be rejected by authors such as Singer and O'Neill.

To end this chapter, it seems worth mentioning that a solution to the division between rights and obligations could be found if we developed certain aspects of our moral life. First, it seems that au-

---

[66] Javier Becerra (*Dictionary of Mexican Legal Terminology*) explains the writ of *amparo* as a "constitutional action alleging the violation of rights committed by the government or a court of law [...] the main purposes of which are: (a) to preserve the rights and freedoms established by the federal constitution against legislative and executive acts, government acts of authority and court decisions, and (b) to preserve local and federal sovereignty in interstate or federal-state disputes [*tr.*].

[67] Article by Jorge Reyes, *Reforma*, section A, p. 4, Mexico City, January 27, 2001; quoting the deputy for the Partido de Acción Nacional (PAN), Buenrostro Díaz.

[68] See J. Elster, *Local Justice*, Cambridge, Cambridge University Press, 1992, p. 153.

[69] Ibid., p. 155.

thors who defend welfare rights and those who argue in favor of obligations towards the poor do not deny the existence of the respective rights and obligations. Perhaps the difference consists in the priority that one or the other may have at the moment of providing arguments to justify any attempt to provide a solution to the problem of extreme poverty. To the degree that we reinforce the need to establish obligations towards the poor, the arguments against welfare rights lose force. Secondly, some of those mentioned above are based on an excessively individualistic consideration of persons. It seems to me that it would be useful to retrieve the notion of citizenship, this would enable us to conceive of individuals as beings who interact in a society, who have rights but also obligations, who develop certain virtues which include those having to do with the well-being of all the individuals who share a given territory. Finally, it is possible to find inspiration in an idea expressed by Jeremy Waldron in the sense that some of the problems facing a distribution on the basis of rights is that these are taken as "guarantees", "valid claims", "demands", established in the articles of a constitution. In Waldron's words:

> ...rights are not to be left at the level of particular Articles in a Declaration. Instead they are to be integrated into a general theory of justice, which will address in a principled way whatever trade-offs and balancing are necessary for their institutionalization in a world characterized by scarcity and conflict.[70]

PROGRESA AND CONSTITUTIONAL RIGHTS

The political constitution of the Mexican Republic establishes certain social rights. Given the PROGRESA attends to health and educational needs, we shall refer to the articles that render these obligations.

Article 3 states that "Every individual has the right to receive education. The Federation—with its states and municipalities—shall impart education at nursery, primary and secondary levels. Primary and secondary education are obligatory...".[71] On the other hand, Article 4 says: "...Every person has the right to protection of health. The Law shall define the bases and means of access to the health services and shall establish the joint responsibility of the Federation

---

[70] J. Waldron, *Liberal Rights*, 1993, p. 33.
[71] *Constitución Política de los Estados Unidos Mexicanos* (February, 1917), p. 7.

and its federated states with regard to public health in general, in accordance with the provisions of Section XVI of Article 73 of this Constitution…".[72] This Section mentions that one of the powers of Congress consists in passing laws on public health.[73]

The advantage of the rights to education and health being constitutional is that any citizen may demand them, and the State has the obligation to guarantee them. Nevertheless, the formulation and fulfillment of these rights presents certain problems. One of these has to do specifically with the very concept of right and the other with putting into practice of social rights, concretely in Mexico.

The difficulty which arises when one tries to put welfare rights into practice lies (as has already been mentioned) in the fact that while it is often clearly specified who is responsible for complying with the obligation in question (in the case of social rights the State), it is at times not possible to comply with the obligation, usually because of a lack of resources.

In the case of Mexico, for example, the right to health is constitutional; nonetheless, it is not easy to determine which are the minimum medical services the State is obliged to provide. As far as education is concerned, while the State may well make an effort to cover in quantitative terms the demand for education, it may not wish to commit itself as regards quality. For example, with the implementation of PROGRESA, school enrollment and requests for medical services have increased considerably; in some communities, however, it has been noted that medical and educational resources are not sufficient to cover the increased demand. It also tends to happen that the medical and educational infrastructures are insufficient to comply with the aims of the program, so that it is necessary for communities to learn to watch over both the functioning of the infrastructure and the conduct of health staff and school teachers. There is thus a need for improved mechanisms to enable the demand to be met.

Another problem concerns the criteria used to determine whether certain members of society have their right to education and health covered. For instance, in Mexico, it is considered that, when a community is served by a federal highway, its education and health needs are met when there is a primary school located at a maximum dis-

---

[72] Ibid., p. 10.
[73] Ibid., p. 61.

tance of five km. and a secondary school and health center within ten km. In the case of communities that are only served by a state highway the respective distances are four and eight km. Some beneficiaries of the program think the distances are overlarge in practice, particularly when one takes into account the difficult geography of many parts of Mexico.

When we deal with the subject of social rights in Mexico, as José Ramón Cossío mentions, we find that two models of the Mexican State have been put forward:

> ...on the one hand, one that limited [the matter] to a merely negative position, one of restriction regarding the exercise of its powers and its active role regarding individuals, and another that, without necessarily ignoring the importance of the liberal order, considered that the legal order ought to include a series of normative contents that might enable certain actions of individuals to be limited with the aim of guaranteeing for others a certain standard of living conditions.[74]

However, Cossío himself, after carrying out a careful study of social rights in Mexico, concludes that: "the rights known as social that appear in the Constitution have, in practice, functioned more as pragmatic political norms that as rights; in other words their interpretation and their application have been more political than legal".[75] Sara Gordon, on the other hand, states that

At the root of these exclusion factors we find a legislation on access to social rights, within the framework of a corporate model, which gives preference to organizations over individuals. [...]. This feature complicates the social recognition of individual and citizens' rights, and favours organized demands made on the State over individual claims.[76]

The conclusion we may reach in this chapter is that, despite all the problems facing the implementation of social rights, we need to exert pressure for these to be fulfilled. One way of doing so is to stimulate the formation of a culture, first of social rights and their scope, and secondly of the mechanisms existing for their satisfaction. It is,

---

[74] J.R. Cossio, "Los derechos sociales como normas programáticas y la comprensión política de la Constitución", pp. 307–308.

[75] Ibid., p. 296.

[76] Sara Gordon, "Poverty and social exclusion in Mexico", International Labor Organization Discussion Paper NO. 93, 1997 (the version cited here is that in Internet: www.ilo.org/public/english/bureau/ inst/papers/1997/dp93/].

therefore, also necessary to provide protection against the ups and downs of the economy. All this must go hand in hand with an insistence on the obligations that both State institutions and citizens must assume towards those who are in a state of poverty. All of this needs to be complemented by an education guided by those virtues that lead us to a concern for our fellow men.

The last two chapters have addressed different criteria for distribution; now we shall set about considering the subject of the motivations that agents responsible for effecting these distributions attribute to the receivers.

IV

UTILITY AND NORMS IN THE STUDY OF POVERTY

> Hunger is hunger; but the hunger that is satisfied
> by cooked meat eaten with a knife and fork dif-
> fers from hunger that devours raw meat with the
> help of hands, nails and teeth.
>
> Karl Marx, *Introduction to* A Contribution
> to a Critique of Political Economy [1]

INTRODUCTION

In Chapter I, I referred to Sir Matthew Hale's interpretation of the
motives that influenced the promulgation of the English Poor Law in
1531.[2] His inquiry into the matter brought to light several reasons for
combating poverty. The first was what Paul Slack has called the
"high-pressure" interpretation, according to which the laws for combating poverty were stimulated by economic circumstances and particularly by the pressure of a population which found itself in a situation of abandonment. The second interpretation put the accent on
changes in public attitudes. The decisive factor was the attempt at
creating a conception regarding what governments could and ought
to do on behalf of the poor. This attitude has been variously thought
to have proceeded from humanism, Protestantism or Puritanism.[3]
While the former motivation for combating poverty arose from a
calculation based on the dangers of the pressure that would be generated by one part of the population on the other, the second responded
to the fulfillment of certain norms which, in this case, had a religious
origin and could be expressed in the form "helping the poor is a
duty".

To deal precisely with the question of the motivations that arise
when we consider the problem of poverty, we ought to distinguish
first of all between those influencing people who implement public
policies and those on the receiving end of such policies. These may

---

[1] Version in Internet (zodiac@io.org).

[2] Paul Slack, *The English Poor Law. 1531–1782*, p. 3.

[3] Ibid.

be totally different, but they may also, in some cases, coincide. The present work, however, is not so much concerned with this kind of difference, but rather with the distinction between actions that respond to norms and those originating in the desire to maximize utility. Perhaps what is most necessary in this context is to understand the concepts of human behavior held by those responsible for implementing public policies. At the root of the problem that concerns us is the difference between a Benthamite and a Kantian philosophical anthropology, or between the tradition inherited from Adam Smith and that from Durkheim,[4] that is, between an economic and a sociological interpretation of behavior.[5]

The theory of rational choice—expressed, for our purposes, as a measure of utility—has made an important contribution to the development of the social sciences, especially the economic and political sciences. Broadly speaking, this theory proposes that an individual, faced with different courses of action, will choose the course which maximizes his expected utility—in other words, that which helps him increase profits and reduce costs. Once agents satisfy the said utility, they will reach a state of well-being; well-being in turn is defined as the achievement of the hoped-for utility.

Some philosophers and social scientists have argued that human behavior cannot be reduced to the satisfaction of utility, and have mentioned the need to incorporate normativity as an element in the explanation of everyday human activity. We can distinguish three positions regarding the relation between behavior explained as maximization of utility and that which responds to norms.

Firstly, there are thinkers who believe that norms themselves can be reduced to rational choice. Thus, when an individual contemplates adhering to or contravening a norm, what weighs over the decision is the consideration of the resulting costs or benefits.

Secondly, there are some who argue that a theory of rational choice cannot be reduced to the maximization of hoped-for utility. They believe such a theory may incorporate forms of behavior regarded as rational, and at the same time recognize the possibility of motivation answering to norms. Of course, in defense of this position

---

[4] See J. Elster, *The Cement of Society*, p. 95.
[5] See M. Hollis, "Rational Man and the Social Sciences", p. 1.

one has to appeal to a different notion of rationality, that of prudential rationality for instance.

Finally, other philosophers are of the opinion that the motivation guiding an agent to act in accordance with norms is different in kind from that followed when acting in accordance with the canons of rational choice. Among the motivations proper to behavior in accordance with norms we find morality, culture and duty.

The repercussions of the above-mentioned discussion are of particular relevance for the study of social policies. For example, some methods of combating poverty have not achieved the hoped-for success because only criteria for assessing maximization of utility, such as income and consumption, have been applied. It has been noted that, while a policy may facilitate an increase in family income or capacity for consumption, men tend to benefit more than women, since the social norm establishes that men as the main breadwinners ought to be better fed. The present chapter thus aims at elucidating two theories that may come into conflict when we try to identify forms of behavior ascribed to agents by those who implement the public policies aimed at the war on poverty.

UTILITY

As has already been mentioned, the chief approach for measuring poverty has been one based on utilitarianism. This method enables us to explain, individually, the behavior of human beings and, at the same time, helps us to predict how the use of goods that a social policy is to distribute can be maximized. George J. Stigler has explained this theory in the following terms: "We believe that man is an animal that maximizes utility—apparently pigeons and rats are too—and so far we have found no information to discover a part of our lives in which to invoke any different aims of behavior".[6] Let us look briefly at the evolution which this theory has undergone.

Amartya Sen distinguishes three different ways of understanding utility: as pleasure, as fulfillment of desires and as choice.[7] He characterizes the utilitarianism based on pleasure as the doctrine by which actions, rules and institutions are justified in terms of human

[6] G.J. Stigler, *El economista como predicador y otros ensayos*, p. 46 (the Spanish version of *The Economist as Preacher* was used as the original was unavailable).
[7] See A. Sen, *The Standard of Living*, p. 7.

happiness and suffering. For those who adopt this way of thinking, agents' choices are judged by the effects or consequences of their actions, and those desires whose satisfaction results in an increase in utility are regard as worthy of being valued. One problem that Sen finds in utilitarianism, as it was defended by classical authors like Jeremy Bentham and John Stuart Mill lies in the inability of this theory to account for the heterogeneity of individual utilities when these are reduced to pleasure and pain. According to Sen, pain can only with difficulty be seen as a negative pleasure; he thus agrees with Dr. Johnson's observation that: "Marriage has many pains, but celibacy has no pleasures".[8] On the other hand the famous remark of John Stuart Mill: "it is better to be Socrates dissatisfied than a pig satisfied" solves nothing, since the reason why we should assign a greater value to the unsatisfied pleasures of Socrates than the satisfied ones of a pig must be sought outside utilitarianism.

On the other hand, Sen discusses the relation between utility and satisfaction of desire. In this respect he quotes Pigou, for whom it was "fair to suppose that most commodities [...] will be desired with intensities proportioned to the satisfactions they are expected to yield".[9] Sen, however, distinguishes between the desire for and the evaluation of a good: "Desire may link closely with valuation, but it is not in itself a valuational activity. [...] There is nothing contradictory in asserting that one does not value something even though one desires it; or [that] one does not value it as strongly as one's desire".[10] Likewise one of the principal problems facing this conception of utilitarianism is that desire explains very little when we talk about intensity and about interpersonal comparisons.[11]

However, the problem of utilitarianism that most concerns Sen lies in the fact that people become accustomed to certain conditions—such as poverty—adjusting their utilities to their real possibilities. It is not merely that a poor person has less to offer for what she desires in comparison with a rich person, but that the intensity of desire itself may become attenuated in response to real possibilities.

---

[8] Ibid., p. 7.

[9] Quoted by A. Sen, *The Standard of Living*, p. 9.

[10] Ibid., pp. 9–10.

[11] Of course, desires, along with beliefs, explain intentional behavior, as Davidson's schema shows. They lack explanatory force, however, where cardinal preferences appear. I am grateful to Carlos Pereda for his insistence in clarifying this idea.

The defeated and the downtrodden come to lack the courage to desire things that others more favorably treated by society desire with easy confidence. The absence of desire for things beyond one's means may not reflect any deficiency of valuing, but only an absence of hope, and a fear of inevitable disappointment.[12]

In interpersonal comparisons, when we refer to well-being, we have no way of comparing the relation of desires to the possibility of satisfying them, and this may generate distortions. The poor, the unemployed, the downtrodden, abused women, etc., may wish for very little and the fulfillment of their desires would represent no success at all, for which reason such desires cannot be dealt with in the same way as the wishes of those who are in a better situation.

Finally, Sen questions the concept of utility as seen in terms of choice. This version takes exclusively ordinal comparisons into account, and holds that if someone chooses x when she has the possibility of choosing y, then we can affirm that x has greater utility for that person than y. The popularity of this approach "may be due to a mixture of an obsessive concern with observability and a peculiar belief that choice (in particular, market choice) is the only human aspect that can be observed".[13] The utilitarian explanation sets out from the idea that each individual maximizes her expected utility, and also from the belief that it is possible to calculate the consequences of taking one decision and leaving another aside— finally from the notion that preferences can be hierarchized, as long as certain conditions are fulfilled.

It is worth noting that the three versions of utilitarianism rest on a certain vision of a rational individual who is able to maximize her utilities, and it is thought that on the basis of certain mathematical functions it is possible to establish a function of social utility.

As we have already seen, some theorists of the social sciences believe that behavior that follows norms can be explained in accordance with the costs and benefits occasioned by following a particular pattern of behavior. To explain such a reductionist position they have had recourse to the notion of the "Nash equilibrium". According to this point of view, social norms are a repetition of a game produced by this "equilibrium". One textbook on microeconomic theory explains the Nash equilibrium by the example of the everyday be-

---

[12] Ibid., pp. 10–11.
[13] Ibid., p. 12.

havior of New Yorkers, who have learned to obey a norm that consists in walking on the right-hand side of the sidewalk, "a convention that is enforced by the fact that any individual who unilaterally deviates from it is sure to severely trampled".[14] To understand the implications of the Nash equilibrium we need to define what is known as the Pareto frontier. A social state is described as optimal in Pareto's sense if, and only if, it is not possible to increase one person's utility without reducing someone else's utility. To understand how, according to Pareto, a transaction is carried out, we shall make use of an explanation provided by Brian Barry.[15] Thus a distribution is regarded as just if a resolution of a dispute between two agents leads to their "mutual advantage", in other words, a "gain over what they would have acquired from a continuation of the conflict". The process for determining a just outcome must be divided in two parts; the first consists in establishing a "nonagreement point" which is the "outcome that the parties will arrive at in the absence of agreement". The second refers to what the parties will have to accept in order to arrive at "a point that preserves their relative advantage at the nonagreement point but is in the set of outcomes that are 'efficient', meaning that one party cannot be made better off without the other being made worse off". In other words the agents move from a situation of disagreement to an efficient situation. The latter is often referred to as the "Pareto frontier". Several authors[16] have reached the conclusion that the problem with the Pareto principle is that in a negotiation a wide range of possibilities (Pareto-optimal points) exist for distribution that meet the requirements of the Pareto frontier, and that the different distributions are made to seem unconnected with the material situations of the agents who carry out the negotiation. A distribution in which one of those taking part in the negotiations ends up with $10.00 and the other $90.00 can be as efficient as one in which both of them have $50.00. Now, Barry[17] explains how Nash tried to resolve the problem of inequality—which is extremely im-

---

[14] "Note that if an outcome is to become a stable social convention, it must be a Nash equilibrium. If it were not, then individuals would deviate from it as soon as it began to emerge". A. Mas-Colell *et al.*, *Microeconomic Theory*, p. 249.

[15] See B. Barry, *Theories of Justice*, p. 10.

[16] B. Barry, op. cit., pp. 13–14; A. Sen, *On Ethics and Economics*, 1992, pp. 31ff; J. Rawls, *A Theory of Justice*, p. 66ff.

[17] See B. Barry, *op. cit.*, pp. 14ff.

portant for the study of poverty—using the criterion of utility pro-posed by Neumann and Morgenstern in order to explain the rational choice that individuals must take in a situation of hypothetical bid-ding. According to these authors, it is possible to consider a pattern of preferences in a group of possible distributions of alternatives. As Kenneth Arrow described the Neumann–Morgenstern theorem: "There is one way [...] of assigning utilities to probability distribu-tions such that behavior is described by saying that the individual seeks to maximize his expected utility".[18]

The utility criterion consists in assigning a utility to the situations in which individuals find themselves at present, as well as those in which they will be once the negotiation is completed. This criterion also allows us to include the information that an agent has regarding the other's utilities. The basic difference between the "Pareto fron-tier" and the "Nash equilibrium" is that in the latter it is necessary to equalize the utility produced by the transaction.

To understand Nash's solution it is useful to underline four ele-ments: 1) that a point of conflict exists, from which the gains to be obtained by negotiating are calculated; 2) that the solution must be obtained along the "Pareto frontier"; 3) it is necessary that a solution exists in which the gains to be obtained if we pass from the "conflict point" to the "Pareto frontier" are stipulated; 4) the information re-quired by the agents in order to carry out the negotiation is reduced to the utilities the negotiation yields to each one of them.

According to Nash, it is possible to arrive at a negotiation if three conditions exist. The first is that "the solution should be invariant with respect to the units in which utility is measured". Nash's solu-tion

...deals with the problem of units by multiplying all the utilities together. (Thus, if we had increased all of the poor man's utilities by a factor of ten, the solution would have come to the same division of the money, because the products of the two men's utilities would have stayed in the same ratio...).[19]

The second is the symmetry of the utilities: if the agents' "utility schedules [...] are identical then the outcome should yield equal utility measured in the same terms as those that made the utility

---

[18] K. Arrow, *Social Choice and Individual Values*, pp. 9–10.
[19] B. Barry, op. cit., pp. 16–17.

schedules identical". The third condition is "the independence of irrelevant alternatives"; this means that an individual chooses between a fixed group of alternatives, which is independent of the existence of other alternatives outside the said group.[20] If the conditions and the solutions are fulfilled, the "Nash principle" represents the best alternative individuals can choose.

The Nash equilibrium sets out to show that the, often repeated, behavior of human beings is due to the calculation of the benefit they expect to obtain by acting in accordance with the behavior of the rest. This is achieved when we are familiar with the strategies followed by the others. For those who believe that human behavior can be reduced to an explanation provided by the theory of rational choice, social norms represent perfect examples of the Nash equilibrium.

One of the problems, however, that arise with Nash's solution is that it is necessary to set a limit on exchanges, since certain goods exist, such as rights that cannot be exchanged.[21] In order to determine the limit between the negotiable and the non-negotiable, we would in turn need a negotiating procedure that does not fulfill the stipulations. Likewise, as we saw in Chapter I, when dealing with credit, the cost of what stands to be lost by individuals in a situation of extreme poverty increases considerably the marginal utility of the transaction.

To explain norms in this way corresponds to the first position referred to at the beginning of this chapter, in other words this is what people think who believe that norms can be reduced to rational choice and that all individuals contemplate a decision to adhere to or infringe a norm in terms of the cost or benefit resulting from the action chosen.

Now, utility has been used to measure the notion of well-being. This notion has been explained as the satisfaction of subjective utilities. And while problems do exist for knowing when these are fully satisfied, it is possible to calculate the minimum necessary for a person to attain a minimum level of well-being; above all in cases of extreme poverty. We can use once more the definition of poverty

---

[20] See K. Arrow, op. cit., p. 26.
[21] See P. Dieterlen, "La negociación y el acuerdo: dos interpretaciones económicas de la justicia", pp. 213–222.

laid down by the European Commission in the first *Community Action Programme to Combat Poverty*: "The poor shall be taken to mean persons, families and groups of persons whose resources (material, cultural and social) are so limited as to exclude them from the minimum acceptable way of life in the [...] States in which they live."[22] And so, as we saw in the first chapter, the methods for measuring poverty have been established in order to detect cases lying below a minimally acceptable level. Nonetheless, as we have already seen, what one understands as minimally acceptable depends on the methodology used.

In general, methods of measuring poverty have placed the accent on limited material conditions. It has been thought that a social policy ought to raise the well-being of individuals, in other words increase the relation between income and consumption, and seek to bring everybody above the poverty line. Individuals will, thanks to such policies, be able to maximize their utilities with the aim of getting as close as possible to a level of well-being. Although the concept of well-being is somewhat controversial, for our purposes, we may adopt the idea—almost universally accepted by economists—of an ordinal measurement used to demonstrate that a system of empirical relations and operations has the same form as a particular system of numerical relations and operations, thus demonstrating that the numerical system has some sense when it is applied to the empirical one. Thus "'well-being' is certainly a quantitative attribute, in the sense that we can sometimes say that one thing makes us better off, or at least as well off, or exactly as well off, as another".[23] It is universally accepted that in cases of single individuals, well-being is measured ordinally. Thus, as was mentioned in Chapter II, well-being is a quantitative attribute in the sense that someone is at least equal to, better, or worse off than someone else. We need, therefore, a method of ordering preferences that takes into account reflexiveness, transitivity and completeness. It is necessary to take into consideration the fact that health and level of education are included in the concept of well-being; but in most economic studies on poverty, these take on a functional character, since they are regarded as im-

---

[22] Cited in Atkinson, "Promise and Performance: Why We Need an Official Poverty Report", p. 126.

[23] James Griffin, *Well-Being*, Oxford, Clarendon Press, 1986, p. 95.

portant to the degree that they contribute to an improvement in individuals' participation in the productive process and thus increase their "living standard".

Now, let us see how this position becomes problematical. First, because we do not always know what maximizes utility. In the case of extreme poverty this is important above all with regard to nutrition and health. Second, the choices a person makes are not easy to observe, and at times, when observed they do not correspond to a clearly maximizing pattern of behavior. Sen considers that this version of utilitarianism rests on the idea that choices depend on our motivations. While the pursuit of well-being, understood as the obtaining of utilities, may be a good motivation, it is not the only possible one. On innumerable occasions we act in accordance with motivations whose consequences have nothing to do with an increase in utility. The suffering of other people may lead us to carry out actions that cannot be described in terms of the notion of utility as choice.[24]

Other critics refer to the way in which agents' preferences are characterized as fixed, static, set apart from the social environment. For some writers, it is impossible to think about preferences without taking into account what Michael Walzer calls "common meanings" shared by a particular social group.[25] Another cause of criticism relates to the ahistorical nature of these approaches. Perhaps it is as important to know the origin and development of certain conflicts as their present characteristics.

When speaking of poverty, an aspect that utilitarian approaches usually overlook is that of resources and the environmental situation in which communities find themselves.

While the quantitative methods used for measuring poverty are similar to that which I have already mentioned, it is important to bear in mind that behind every method there is a particular history, and that often the decision to use one or another is a personal choice. It is as well to remember Amartya Sen's warning about the difficulty for

---

[24] See Ibid., p. 13. A. Sen, *Bienestar, justicia y mercado*, p. 89; and "Capacity and Well-Being", p. 37.
[25] See *Spheres of Justice*. In this work Walzer criticizes individualist positions stating that it is in accordance with the nature of the society of which we are members that we produce and distribute our actions, thoughts, goods, etc.

positivist economics to find ways of describing facts objectively since these are always permeated by value judgments.[26]

The above-mentioned methods for measuring poverty represent an effort to detect the sector of the population that is in a state of poverty. Generally, they consist of quantitative indicators of considerable usefulness for designing policies to combat poverty used mainly by economists and demographers. In countries like Mexico, however, with a large rural population, It may make sense, while applying methods that use quantitative indicators for measuring poverty, to consider also those behavioral patterns that respond to traditions, cultural features and social characteristics. As Julio Boltvinik has remarked:

> From the biological point of view, the human need for food is absolutely comparable to that of certain species of animals. Nonetheless, as the passage from Marx referring to the different types of hunger suggests, from the viewpoint of the satisfaction of human needs, nutrition must be seen as a complex phenomenon, affected not only by what is eaten but by the ways in which food is prepared and consumed. What is eaten, how it is prepared, and in whose company, are all elements that form part of human food needs.[27]

As I interpret Boltvinik, the behavior of individuals must be explained in some way by recourse to the utility provided them by particular goods, foods for instance; but of even greater importance are the social and traditional details surrounding their consumption; in the same way, when studying poverty, it is advisable to study the behavior of people as a following of "norms". For the effects of the present work, I shall refer to "social" norms and, following the work of Jon Elster, who resists reducing them to the theory of rational choice, I shall try to characterize them.

SOCIAL NORMS

Behavior ruled by norms is governed by notions of the type: "do this" and "don't do that", and by more complex propositions such as "if you do Y, then also do X", or "if others do Y, then do Y", or "if it is good for anybody to do X, then do X". Martin Hollis has expressed this through the following syllogism applied to citizens who

---

[26] See A. Sen, "Description as Choice", p. 433.
[27] Julio Boltvinik, "Conceptos y medidas de la pobreza", p. 37.

have duties. The initial premise affirms: it is required that citizens fulfill their duty; the second states: a citizen's duty is to do X; and the conclusion establishes: citizens must do X.[28] This point of view suggests that human beings do not always act as maximizers of utility but rather as essentially social beings localized in a schema of positions and functions. In the case of the syllogism we have just set forth, the role played out by human beings is that of the "citizen" with duties to fulfill irrespective of the utility that this produces. Sociological man is not an egoist, and his behavior, far from depending on selected incentives, turns upon the pursuit of a schema of positions favoring a process of socialization.[29]

The difficulty I identify with this approach is that of characterizing social norms and differentiating them from moral ones, and above all from other forms of behavior governed by traditions, customs and usages.

According to Jon Elster,[30] for a norm to be social it must be (a) shared with other people and (b) reinforced by disapproval or approval. A characteristic of social norms is that the members of the community show approval or disapproval by means of a sanction. Now, in order to distinguish a norm as "social" it is important to recognize what type of sanction it produces. According to Elster, the characteristic of social norms is that they leave an imprint in the mind due to the emotions, such as shame, guilt and anxiety, that are produced when someone violates them or is discovered violating them.[31] We might say that, when a social norm is broken, an internal sanction is produced that lies in the negative emotions, and an external sanction that may vary from mild repudiation to being "sent to Coventry" or even to total expulsion from the community. An example of the former in Mexico is the feeling of guilt that may be generated internally if one abandons the dead by neglecting to place an "offering" for them; of the latter, the expulsions from the village of San Juan Chamula in Chiapas of a group of indigenous protestants "because they refused to cooperate with the traditions".[32]

---

[28] See Martin Hollis, op. cit., p. 7.

[29] Ibid., p. 9.

[30] J. Elster, *The Cement of Society*. p. 99.

[31] Op. cit., p. 100.

[32] See Rosa Isabel Estrada Martínez, *El problema de las expulsiones en las comunidades de los altos de Chiapas y los derechos humanos*, p. 63.

It is necessary then to establish differences between moral and social norms and, in consequence, to the need to differentiate between moral and non-moral emotions. As for social norms, these constitute hypothetical imperatives while moral norms are of a categorical nature. Nevertheless, Elster mentions that when we act in accordance with a social norm, we do not calculate the consequences, in other words these are unconditional, and in cases when they are conditional they are not oriented towards the future, in other words in this sense they are also categorical. This enables us to distinguish social norms form conventions. According to Elster, the latter rest on the consequences in a substantive manner and are like the traffic regulations of social life.[33] For instance, if I fail to use the knives and forks "the way you're supposed to" at a dinner, it is possible that I will not be invited again.

In his book *Alchemies of the mind*, Elster provides a more detailed explanation of social norms. According to Elster, these have four characteristic features. First, they are not oriented by the consequences of the action. At their simplest they take the form of unconditional imperatives: "Always wear black at funerals". These may contrast with imperatives oriented towards consequences, such as the statement: "Always wear black in strong sunshine".[34] In a more complex form, norms can be conditional imperatives that make the action depend on past behavior, whether one's own or that of others, but in no way on future consequences. The norms of reciprocity have this form: help those who help you and do harm to those who harm you. Second, social norms are shared with other members of society or with a significant subgroup of society. All members know that they are subject to norms and know that all know this. Thirdly, given that all share the same norms, members of the group can strengthen these norms by sanctioning those who violate them. The range of sanctions can vary considerably, from ostracism to persecution. Finally, norms are also upheld by the internalized emotion of shame.

For Elster, although this approach is deceptive, this does not render it incorrect. This is due to the fact that it gives the impression that the strengthening of norms is over-determined by two sufficient causes: external sanctions and internalized emotions. If this were the

---

[33] Ibid., p. 101.
[34] J. Elster, *Alchemies of the Mind*, p. 145.

case, the explanation of norms by reference to a system of material sanctions would be incomplete rather than false: the explanation would be incomplete since sanctions do not work by the imposition of losses upon those persons at whom they are aimed. When someone refuses to deal with a person who has violated a social norm, he may suffer a financial loss. More important still, he may see the sanction as a vehicle of the emotions of pleasure or displeasure and suffer shame as a result. The material aspect of the sanction, which is important, refers to the cost for the sanctioner of imposing the penalty on the person against whom the sanction is directed, and not to how much it may cost the latter to suffer the penalty. The more it costs us to reject dealings with someone, the stronger will the rejected person feel the contempt that lies behind the refusal, and all the more acute will thus be the sense of shame. According to Elster the phrase "this hurts me more than it hurts you" may serve to increase the punishment, not diminish it.[35] Although there may be heavy costs for the sanctioner, these often intensify the cost to the sanctioned. According to Elster it is the cost to the sanctioner that occasions some type of emotion in the sanctioned. The person who is the focus of rejection thinks that the others see him as bad enough to be avoided, whatever the consequences.

> The emotional content of sanctions was recognized by Aristotle, who wrote that "shame is the imagination of disgrace, in which we shrink from the disgrace itself and *not from its consequences*".[36]

It is important to emphasize the force that Elster attributes to the word "consequence". At times he relates it directly to the calculation which belongs to the theory of rational choice. It seems to me that another way of understanding it derives from the hypothetical imperative. Kant expresses it as follows: "Hypothetical imperatives declare a possible action to be practically necessary as a means to the attainment of something else that one wills (or that one may will)".[37] The consequences of an action are desired and therefore the action is carried out; we would seem to be facing a case of prudential reason. Let us remember that when we refer to prudential reason, the percep-

---

[35] Ibid., p. 146.
[36] Loc. cit. The quotation is from Aristotle, *Rhetoric,* 1348a.
[37] E. Kant, *Groundwork of the Metaphysic of Morals*, p. 82.

tion of the goodness of the state of things in the future is what causes the action. We are not talking about a calculation of costs and benefits. For instance, we might say that the indigenous protestants referred to above could have chosen to cooperate with the traditions because to continue to live in their community was desirable, and not by a simple calculation.

Of course, a difference exists between social and legal norms. The latter are characterized by the fact that their sanctions are, in some way, written down. Likewise, the motivations of agents to follow them acquire importance to the degree that the punishment is increased or diminished. As Rolando Tamayo explains in an introduction to a text by Hart:

> Law is differentiated from other systems of social norms in having as a characteristic feature the fact of being both institutional and systemic. It is institutional because its entities (primary and secondary norms) are created and applied by social instances having authority; it is systemic, because it depends on the interrelation of these two types of norms.[38]

Another important distinction is that which exists between "customs and usages" and social norms. For Elster, the distinction can be made despite its tenuousness. Tradition can be understood as an unconscious way of repeating and imitating, in the present, what our forbears did in the past. Tradition is subject to a process of inertia; it embodies a corpus of limitations resulting from an accumulative process. Perhaps an important difference between such traditions and social norms lies in the fact that a distancing from or adoption of a tradition occasions neither sanctions of an external nor an internal nature.

While I am conscious of the fact that the discussion of "community rights" in Mexico has been based on the importance of incorporating "customs and usages" in the various legislations, I believe that a philosophical approach can distinguish between actions that form part of a tradition, such as social norms, infringement of which may lead to changes in the communities, and those which simply constitute a way of imitating what predecessors did in the past.

---

[38] R. Tamayo "Ensayo preliminar", in H.L.A. Hart, *Post scríptum al concepto de derecho*, p. xxiv.

Nonetheless, in order to show that the difference is not always very clear, I shall refer to an example based on an idea that appears in *The Wealth of Nations*. Adam Smith tells us:

> By necessaries I understand not only the commodities which are indispensably necessary for the support of life, but whatever the custom of the country renders it indecent for creditable people, even the lowest order, to be without. [...] Custom [...] has rendered leather shoes a necessary of life in England. The poorest creditable person of either sex would be ashamed to appear in public without them.[39]

I should like to underline that two conclusions are to be drawn from the text I have just quoted. On the one hand, it seems that Smith confuses tradition and social norm, since if the fact of not having leather shoes produces a feeling of shame, this is due to the fact that the use of such articles comes from a social norm and not from a "custom". On the other hand, it seems that the difference between custom and social norm is not always very clear, at least as far as emotions are concerned.

This problem arises in Rousseau when, in his *Social Contract*, he states that there is a kind of law

> ...which is not graven on tablets of marble or brass, but on the hearts of citizens. This forms the real constitution of the State, takes on every day new powers, when other laws decay or die out, restores them or takes their place [...]. I am speaking of morality, of custom, above all of public opinion; a power unknown to political thinkers, on which none the less success in everything else depends..[40]

H.L.A. Hart, on the other hand, establishes a difference between what we call social norms and what we refer to as uses and customs. According to Hart, it is necessary to abandon the apparently simple idea that a social norm or rule[41] exists because a group of people, or most of them, behave similarly in certain types of circumstances.[42] To establish the distinction that exists between a form of behavior that follows a custom and one that is governed by social norms he

---

[39] Cited by Amartya Sen, in "Poor, Relatively Speaking", p. 333.

[40] J.J. Rousseau, *The Social Contract and Discourses*, Everyman's Library, Dent, London, 1973 1964, p. 394.

[41] The words "norm" and "rule" will be used without distinction.

[42] H.L.A. Hart, *The Concept of Law*, p. 9.

refers to the difference in Great Britain between taking tea at five o'clock and standing to attention when the National Anthem is played. According to Hart the idea that most people generally do these things is not enough to establish the difference. He tells us that "mere convergence in behavior between members of a social group may exist (all may regularly drink tea at breakfast or go weekly to the cinema) and yet there may be no rule *requiring* it."[43] Hart inquires into the difference between habitual convergent behavior in a group, and rules expressed by the words "have to" and "must". In his opinion, in cases of "mere group habits [...] deviations are not met with punishment or even reproof". This would be the case, however, when the rules require a particular conduct; nonetheless, in the case of non-legal norms, the hostile reaction to the deviation "is not organized or definite in character.[44]

Hart explains an additional element, apart from the non-organized censure of those who deviate, which helps us to distinguish between a norm and a simple habit. In part, his explanation coincides with that of Elster, and has to do with the fact that the predictable reaction to deviations consists in "our powerful 'feelings' of compulsion to behave in accordance with the rule and to act against those who do not".[45] This explanation has recourse to the existence of an emotion or a feeling when a deviation from a rule takes place.

Hart reinforces his thesis on social norms by affirming that these are "more than convergent habits or regularities of behavior; they are taught, and efforts are made to maintain them; they are used in criticizing our own and other people's behavior in the characteristic normative vocabulary".[46] A social rule imposes obligations when there is insistence on people's acting in accordance with it; likewise, pressure is exercised on those who deviate from it. Rules can have a purely customary origin, in other words their application may lack a centrally organized system of punishments to deal with transgressions; likewise, social pressure may take on merely the form of a generally disseminated critical or hostile reaction which does not go as far as the imposition of physical sanctions; finally, application

---

[43] Ibid., p. 9.
[44] Ibid., p. 10.
[45] Ibid., p. 11.
[46] Ibid. p. 86.

may be limited to verbal manifestations of disapproval or invocations of respect by individuals *vis-à-vis* the violated rule. As Elster also mentions, the imposition of social norms "may depend heavily on feelings of shame, remorse and guilt".[47]

Social norms are also important "because they are believed to be necessary to the maintenance of social life or some highly prized feature of it.[48]

Having analyzed the thinking of Elster and Hart, we may identify three characteristics that distinguish social norms and rules from what we usually call customs or usages. First of all their violation sets off emotions such as shame; secondly, a sanction exists that is not organized and which has no specific manner of execution; thirdly, a deviation from the norm tends to vitiate the preservation of the group's social life.

As can be seen, social norms have attained considerable importance within the study of poverty, since they are rules susceptible of being reinforced without the members of a community having the need to use coercion. They are strategies of behavior since every person who follows them behaves as if all members of the community were guided by them.[49]

Partha Dasgupta[50] has explained the importance of such norms particularly in those countries with a large rural population. In his studies of poverty, this writer has observed that the various types of exchange—even economic ones—do not always take place for reasons of utility. He sets out to examine what it is that upholds systems of reciprocity and what motivates people to fulfill their obligations even where the legal system does not operate, and suggests three answers. The first has to do with the characteristics of the rural communities themselves, which possess their own power and authority structures embodied in village elders, caciques, priests, or those with merely a greater hold on economic resources. Such structures are effective as long as "all others accept the structure of authority"; when this is the case "each has an incentive to accept it". The second

---

[47] Loc. cit.

[48] Ibid., p. 87

[49] See P. Dasgupta, *Environmental and resource economics in the world of the poor*, p. 12.

[50] See P. Dasgupta, *An Inquiry into Well-Being and Destitution*, Oxford, Clarendon Press, 1996, pp. 206–212.

answer is found in the internalization of reciprocity. This is a process taking place over time, beginning in early childhood and inculcated by a life in common that molds upbringing through experiences of rewards and punishments. The third answer sees social norms as "injunctions on behavioral strategies". Such injunctions "must be accepted by members of society generally" if they are to attain the status of social norms. When individuals find themselves in situations that tend to repeat, norms become established and maintained even without being internalized. All that is needed is a context in which individuals know each other, are familiar with the natural and social environment in which they exist and expect to continue interacting under similar circumstances; the basis for all this is common knowledge and belonging. Elster had argued in favor of internalization as the "central means" by which norms are sustained (with the implication that this third answer would not work). Dasgupta disagrees, offering this kind of categorization of social norms as a useful basis for further research, since it "has the virtue that it enables us to explain social norms in terms of localized interests, and ecological and technological constraints".[51]

Now it is necessary to state that, while the existence of social norms seems to provide its own rationale for the tendency of individuals to behave in accordance with them, we also need a criterion that would allow us to distinguish between the norms we ought to foster and those we need to eliminate. Perhaps the answer is to be found in democratic practice. In certain communities norms have given rise to situations of alarming inequality. In Mexico for example it has been observed that certain homes subsist below the poverty line and that it is therefore necessary to attend to them. However, the different degrees of poverty existing within particular families has been overlooked. Inequality between men and women is due to the imposition of certain norms: for instance that idea that women need to eat less than men, or that in case of a mother's absence it is the girls, and not the boys, that must stay away from school in order to look after the smallest children. Perhaps the values of democracy, with their commitment to equality, are a parameter for distinguishing the norms that a policy should respect from those it should try to change; for example the Fourth Article of the Mexican Constitution

---

[51] Ibid., p. 212.

sets forth that "Male and female are equal before the law. The law protects the organization and development of the family". Thus social policies must contribute to ensuring the disappearance of the "norm of the inequality of women". Finally, as the sociologist John Heritage states: "The norms through which situations and their component actions are recognized are to be understood not as rigid templates, but as elastic and revisable resources which are adjusted and altered over the course of their application to concrete contexts".[52]

Finally, I should like to point out that the two kinds of explanations—by interest and by norms—lead to a collision between an economic vision of poverty, an anthropological and a sociological one. Nevertheless, if we wish to study poverty and apply measures to combat it, we need to take them all into account. To ignore any one of them may lead to a failure in the design and implementation of public policies designed to eradicate it.

One way of combining the social and the economic approaches would be to regard well-being as not only a subjective measure of utility but as the conditions that make it possible for a person to realize her life plans. The appropriate concept for dealing with well-being as an objective element is, once again, "need". From this point of view we can characterize two categories of need: instrumental needs, which are those things we require in order to attain our life plans; and basic needs, which are things we require simply to continue to exist as human beings.[53] For instance, we need food to survive and even when we may, in certain circumstances, prefer not to live, survival is, in general, one of the inbuilt aims of human nature and not something subject to choice. Normally, we speak of human needs as if they were not only basic but absolute; this means that human beings need food, health, a roof, not in order to achieve something else but simply to make life tolerable. Taking this idea of needs into account we can define well-being, at least the conception of this that we are going to use as an interpersonal measure of moral judgments, as the level at which needs are satisfied.[54] Thus basic needs are those that serve all purposes, irrespective of the goals that are

---

[52] John C. Heritage, "Ethnomethodology" in *Social Theory Today*, Polity Press, 1987, p. 247.
[53] Griffin, op. cit., p. 41.
[54] Ibid., p. 42.

chosen. The relevance of this statement is that we do not relate needs with choices, but with that which is characteristic of human existence. Individuals normally choose their life plans; they do not, however, choose what they regard as necessary in order to carry out a life plan once decided on.

While the word need, as we saw in the previous chapter, is somewhat vague, and although the line between basic needs and those which are not basic may change, a certain rationality is apparent in the process of establishing them. Generally, it is not difficult, particularly in countries where a large number of people live in extreme poverty, to draw up a list of basic needs.

What we are trying to achieve when we include the idea of objective well-being is to incorporate a measure that cannot be reduced exclusively to criteria of utility and that can be included in behavior that follows norms. It is important to emphasize that for the study of poverty, as was mentioned above, following Boltvinik, needs are always satisfied in ways that form part of a context of normativity. The study of norms may serve as an index of the way in which different groups satisfy their basic needs. For example, a community may think that men have more need of health services that women, since the former contribute directly to the production process. This, of course, depends on the role assigned to women. Many elements of behavior governed by a system of social norms are at a far remove from the satisfaction of basic needs. Now, to take seriously behavior that "follows norms" would commit us to orient public policies for combating poverty in the direction of Michael Walzer's proposal: "that, tax money should be fed into the ethnic communities to help in the financing of bilingual and bicultural education, and of group-oriented welfare services".[55] Objective well-being, in one sense, can be adjusted to the norms established by a group, for instance by finding the most appropriate way of satisfying the basic needs. However, attention to basic needs can also result in changes in certain norms of behavior. For example, in patriarchal societies, policies exist that are aimed at combating poverty, where the primary objective is to improve the conditions of women. Such policies, as has already been mentioned, will contribute to changes in certain norms and to a closer approach to the democratic ideal of equality between men and

---

[55] Michael Walzer, "Pluralism: A Political Perspective", p. 149.

women. Policies that try to combat poverty by altering certain norms of behavior will be successful to the degree that people do not feel shame or fear of social sanction, nor think that their community is being threatened in some way.

Amartya Sen has also offered a thesis to demonstrate the importance for the study of poverty not only of the social norms imposed by the community but also of personal choice. He believes that agents' motivations arise from multiple causes among which not only utility but also prudence, and moral and social norms stand out. He does, however, criticize those positions that exaggerate the weight of social norms. These criticisms are expressed with absolute clarity in a lecture entitled "Reason Before Identity". The first criticism has to do with the concept of social identity and the second with that of choice. According to Sen, it is useful to consider "two different ways in which social identity can be important: its, on the other hand, "may be a fundamental part of an adequate formulation of any idea of the social good, and even of the definition of the scope and limits of social interest and appropriate behavior. [...]. In any diagnosis of the social good a question arises regarding who would be included in this exercise of aggregation, and this task cannot be separated from the practice of social identification".[56]

According to Sen, it is not difficult to see that "outlining leaves room for choice and reasoning". Besides, for the purpose of drawing a "particular map of the division into groups, one can ask two questions. First, a person could ask whether lines can be redrawn on the same map. Must a person regard himself, for instance, as European and not simply Italian" (or in the Mexican case, indigenous rather than simply Tarahumara, or a Mexican from Chiapas rather than, exclusively, an indigenous Catholic or Protestant from San Juan Chamula)? According to Sen, these are "substantial matters that deserve discussion".[57] Secondly, since "there are different maps and different procedures for dividing people", is it not possible for people to define their identity simultaneously in different ways—as, for example: woman, indigenous, Mexican, from Chiapas, and so on? Sometimes conflicts arise as "alternative identities [...] compete for

---

[56] A. Sen, "La razón antes que la identidad", p. 14. (The version used here was the Spanish translation of this lecture as the original was not available at the time).
[57] Ibid., p. 15.

importance in a given context"; such conflicts of identity become linked to conflicts of interests regarding important matters and easily unleash tragic events. It seems to me that this problem has arisen in Mexico in communities whose members have everything in common except for their religious beliefs.

The fact that individuals are faced with a variety of different possible ways off defining their identity leads on to the possibility of choice. However, as Sen notes, the conceptions that underline the norms dictated by a community often tend to acquire a persuasive power, making definitive communal identity a matter of personal realization or discovery and not one of choice. Michael Sandel expresses this point of view when he states that "the community describes just what [people] *have* as fellow citizens, but also what they *are*; not a relation they choose (as in a voluntary association), but a common tie they discover; not merely an attribute, but an element constitutive of their identity".[58] Sen, on the other hand, finds it difficult to imagine that we really cannot make a substantial choice between identities—that identity is merely something we simply have to "discover".

Now, it is important to make some clarifications regarding the concept of choice. First, it does not follow from the fact that choice is important that any choice we make must be definitive and permanent. In reality, our own loyalties and definitions often oscillate. Second, the possibilities of choice are restricted. There are limits to what we can choose to identify with, and perhaps even clearer limits when it comes to persuading others to accept us as something different from what they already consider us to be. Third, it is obvious that we *can* "discover" our identity in the sense of verifying that we have a connection to a point of origin that we were previously unaware of. We discover many things about ourselves, but "recognizing this is not the same as reducing identity to a matter of discovery, even when a person discovers something very important about herself. In any case, one still has to face questions of choice".[59]

Sen's opinion with regard to certain positions that affirm the priority of social norms and customs as against choice are found in the following passage:

---

[58] Quoted by Sen, Ibid., p. 15.
[59] Ibid., p. 16.

If some of us, nowadays, continue to show ourselves suspicious in view of communitarian conceptions, for all their attractive aspects—for example, the focus on solidarity within a group and on the beneficent effect towards others within the group—there are historical reasons for this. In fact, solidarity within a group can go hand in had with discord between groups. I think that similar irrational changes of identity have taken place and will continue to do so in different parts of the world [...]. There is something deeply debilitating about denying the possibility of choosing when such choice exists, since this is equivalent to an abdication of the responsibility to consider and value how one ought to think and with what one ought to identify. It is equivalent to being a victim of the irrational changes of a putative knowledge based on the false belief that identity is something that must be discovered and accepted, rather than something to be examined and scrutinized.[60]

We may conclude that when we study a social phenomenon it is fundamental to take into account the fact that norms cause forms of behavior, even when it is not very clear how they do so and that they are not merely rationalizations of the principle of utility. To understand this is to broaden the field of explanation of the actions of men and women, and thus make it possible to design policies that really enable us to combat the innumerable cases of extreme poverty that affect countries like Mexico in all their dimensions.

THE IMPORTANCE OF UTILITIES AND NORMS
IN THE APPLICATION OF PROGRESA

As I have already mentioned, the conception of individuals as maximizers of utility has been applied by certain economists who have studied the impact of the PROGRESA program; it has been mainly sociologists and anthropologists, on the other hand, who have taken into account the behavioral norms of families who have received assistance from the Program. We would do well to remember that in one of the evaluations consumption was used as a means of measuring well-being. Some of those who evaluated the program commented that:

As economists we tend to place the emphasis on means of measuring poverty based on consumption [...] [This method] is highly valued since while complying with all the desired axioms in measurements of poverty [it also] contains a

---

[60] Ibid., p. 17.

parameterα that can be set in accordance with the sensibilities of society regarding the distribution of income among the poor."[61]

We might conclude from the above statement that the evaluation of the Program's impact is based on the possibility it affords individuals to spend more money.

It is important to mention that quantitative means of evaluation are necessary but not sufficient for judging the impact of a public policy program. As was mentioned in Chapter I, it is necessary to improve the economic situation of those who are in conditions of extreme poverty, but we also need to take into account the impact that PROGRESA has had on the behavior of individuals who—while anxious to increase their capacity for consumption—adhere to certain patterns of behavior. In this connection I refer to an anthropological study of the effects of PROGRESA on certain communities.[62]

This study affirms that indigenous peasant communities have a system of egalitarian redistribution that operates via various mechanisms of social control, that the Program is generating disturbances in the internal order, and that the traditional communal authorities are expressing disagreement with the externally imposed vertical procedure. The study also notes that ties of social cohesion are being fragmented by external decisions, which generate conflicts in the extended family, between different neighborhoods, or between the promoters and the non-beneficiaries. Another problem consists in the fact that forms of traditional leadership and government have not been taken into consideration, and that this is likely to lead to future conflict.[63]

It is acknowledged, however, that, despite the deliberate targeting of women as a basic mechanism for promoting change, they continue to accept a submissive role with regard to men. Nonetheless, their economic dependence has been modified. Women have won new spaces for activity in the community and constitute a living organization that is being mobilized towards a common purpose.

---

[61] E. Skoufias, B. Davis and J. Behrman, "Evaluación del sistema de selección de familias beneficiarias en PROGRESA", p. 85.

[62] Salomón Nahmad, Tania Carrasco, Sergio Sarmiento, "Acercamiento etnográfico y cultural sobre el impacto del Programa PROGRESA en doce comunidades de seis estados de la República", pp. 62–109.

[63] Ibid., p. 107.

In some communities this has brought about an incipient change in self-esteem; women are no longer merely housewives who remain at home awaiting their families; now they are known as "PROGRESA women". They are united because the program makes it possible for them to organize themselves.[64]

It seems to me that a public policy that changes certain norms of behavior with the aim of bringing people closer to the state of equality stipulated by the Constitution has a high probability of success. The success will, however, depend to some degree on the commitment of those who implement such policies not to trample over the social norms of the communities, as long as these do not hinder the approach to more democratic forms of conviviality.

We should remember that social norms, such as Hart defines them, must contribute to preserving something of value in social life. If a change takes place in a social norm it must occur in pursuit of something even more valuable. In the case of PROGRESA the intention was to help families to find their way out of the state of extreme poverty and to help women to achieve a situation of greater equality.

Since we set out from the fact that equality is an ideal that is worth seeking, the following chapter will examine some matters related to this ideal.

---

[64] Ibid., pp. 92–93.

V

EQUALITY

Imagine no possessions
I wonder if you can
No need for greed or hunger
A brotherhood of man
Imagine all the people
Sharing all the world
                    John Lennon

INTRODUCTION

In the introduction to this book I mentioned that the problems of poverty, treated from a philosophical point of view, have an egalitarian liberal theory as their backcloth. This means that a redistribution of resources whose beneficiaries are those members of a society who are in a situation of extreme poverty must respect certain liberties and, more concretely, the rights of all individuals belonging to that society. The present chapter will deal briefly with the subject of liberty. Nevertheless, as the problem of distribution is intimately related to that of equality, I shall undertake an analysis of a number of concepts that set out to explain the latter, since, as we have already seen, the criteria of distribution are related to the achievement of a less unequal society. However, it is possible to conceive of a society that is egalitarian but at the same time unjust, for example one in which all members are equally poor. It could also happen that policies of combating poverty are applied that entail as a consequence an increase in inequality.

The subject of the relation between freedom and equality takes on importance in theories of distributive justice, since these attempt to respect individual liberties while at the same time seeking the principles or the criteria for distribution of scarce goods and services in order to identify those who most need them.

As was mentioned in the first chapter of this book, when dealing with matters concerning distribution of resources it is impossible to overlook the importance of the work of Rawls. For this reason, it is worth recalling that this author proposes the following principles of justice. The first states that "each person has an equal right to the most extensive scheme of equal basic liberties compatible with a similar scheme of liberties for all"; and the second that "social and economic inequalities are to satisfy two conditions: they must be *a)* to the greatest benefit of the least advantaged members of society; and *b)* attached to offices and positions open to all under conditions of fair equality of opportunity".[1] The second principle, called that of difference, is that which commits us to an egalitarian conception of society. But, as was mentioned above, first we shall examine briefly the concept of liberty.

LIBERTY

According to Rawls, the basic liberties, of which the first principle of justice speaks, are the following:

> political liberty (the right to vote and to be eligible for public office), together with freedom of speech and assembly; liberty of conscience and freedom of thought; freedom of the person* along with the right to hold (personal) property; and freedom from arbitrary arrest and seizure as defined by the concept of the rule of law. These liberties are all required to be equal by the first principle, since citizens of a just society are to have the same basic rights.[2]

These liberties may be defined as "negative", in other words, they place limits on what the State and other members of society are permitted to do to us, for instance subjecting us to arbitrary arrest, preventing us from expressing our ideas, or meeting freely.

Perhaps the most famous essay on freedom is that written by Isaiah Berlin.[3] In this essay, Berlin defines negative freedom as the area in which a man may act without being obstructed by others. He tells us:

---

[1] J. Rawls, "Social Unity and Primary Goods", pp. 161–162.
[2] J. Rawls, *A Theory of Justice*, p. 61. The Spanish edition used by this author includes, after the word *person*, the following phrases: "...which includes liberty in the face of psychological oppression, physical aggression and dismemberment (integrity of the person)" *(tr.)*.
[3] Isaiah Berlin, "Two Concepts of Liberty", pp. 141–152.

> If I am prevented by other persons from doing what I could otherwise do, I am to
> that degree unfree; and if this area is contracted by other men beyond a certain
> minimum, I can be described as being coerced, or, it may be, enslaved.[4]

For Berlin, to be free in this sense means not to suffer the interference of others. The greater the area in which a person can act without suffering interference, the broader is his freedom. Nonetheless, human beings have interests that come into conflict, pursue goals or purposes that may clash with those of others; it is thus necessary that the free actions of human beings are regulated by a system of laws. These have been made to protect the exercise of individual liberties and enable them to coexist.

Practically all those authors referred to as "liberal", from classics like Locke and Mill to contemporary thinkers such as Rawls, Nozick and Dworkin, uphold the importance for members of a society of the protection of such liberties by the State. The protection of liberties is a basic function of the minimal or "night-watchman" State.

Liberty becomes more problematic when we consider its positive sense. This, as we saw in Chapter II in connection with Sen's notion of capacity, is defined as follows:

> The 'positive' sense of the word 'liberty' derives from the wish on the part of the
> individual to be his own master. I wish my life and decisions to depend on my-
> self, not on external forces of whatever kind. I wish to be the instrument of my
> own, not of other men's acts of will. I wish to be a subject, not an object; to be
> moved by reasons, by conscious purposes which are my own, not by causes
> which affect me, as it were, from outside. I wish to be somebody, not nobody; a
> doer—deciding, not being decided for, self-directed and not acted upon by exter-
> nal nature or by other men as if I were a thing, or an animal, or a slave incapable
> of playing a human role, that is of conceiving goals and policies of my own and
> realizing them..[5]

As has already been mentioned, while agreement exists between liberal thinkers regarding the need to protect negative liberties, the same does not hold for positive freedoms, since for people to be in a position to exercise them it is necessary for the State to intervene to a greater extent than in a merely protective sense. It must implement certain policies for human beings to be capable of exercising positive

---

[4] Ibid., pp. 141–142.
[5] Ibid., p. 140.

liberties; for example, while, according to the concept of negative freedom, the State has the obligation to protect freedom of expression, where positive liberty is concerned, it also has to implement adequate measures—in the field of education for instance—so that individuals have the capacity to exercise such freedom.

Discussion regarding the two concepts of freedom is intimately related to that which has taken place between the defenders of rights in the strict sense and those who support the idea of the Welfare State, as we saw in Chapter III. This controversy has direct repercussions for the conflict between the possibility of exercising certain liberties and the implementation of egalitarian policies. Ronald Dworkin and other thinkers maintain that certain measures for reducing inequality and poverty that are effected through the implementation of redistributive taxes and laws on minimum wages, are tyrannical.[6] On the other hand, the defenders of equality insist that the predominance of the value of liberty in our societies, including economic freedom, has contributed substantially to increasing inequality. Other thinkers, like Dworkin himself, acknowledge that the market—the distributive mechanism *par excellence*—creates great inequalities because individuals do not enter into exchanges with the same initial goods and services at their command, and thus the results of such exchanges are unequal.[7]

Egalitarian liberal philosophers, on the other hand, see both freedom and equality as political ideals that can coexist in a political system; this is due to the fact that—as we shall see further on—equality implies an involuntary situation but also leaves a space for individual decisions.

Nonetheless, before arriving at this conclusion it seems pertinent to consider at least two arguments against equality expressed by authors who deny its legitimacy as a social principle. The first refers to the priority weighting that ought to be accorded freedom and the second to the motivation that some thinkers believe underlies demands for equality.

---

[6] See Ronald Dworkin, "Do Liberty and Equality Conflict?", p. 39.
[7] See Ronald Dworkin, "Liberalism", p. 131.

The main argument against equality is probably one which concerns the apparent relation between equality and distributive justice, in other words with the mechanisms and criteria of distribution and redistribution that are necessary to attain a less unequal society. On studying the concept of redistributive justice, however, we find that the relation existing between the latter and equality is at times confused. While no few philosophers and economists have tried to explain and demonstrate that any theory of justice implies, of necessity, an idea of equality, there are others who think that the two things are in reality unconnected. The latter subscribe to the thesis that a society forced to be egalitarian may turn out to be extremely unjust. If we look closely at this point of view we may discern two basic attitudes in the work of those thinkers who deny the value of equality. The first emphasizes that equality strikes precisely against people's freedom of choice. The second affirms that the real motivation behind demands for equality is a hidden passion known as envy.

The first attitude holds that justice is foreign to equality since any principle of distribution prevents human beings from exercising their liberty. One of the principal defenders of this thesis is Robert Nozick. As a starting point, this author offers the following rules for considering the justice of distribution in holdings:

1. A person who acquires a holding in accordance with the principle of justice in acquisition is entitled to that holding.
2. A person who acquires a holding in accordance with the principle of justice in transfer, from someone else entitled to the holding, is entitled to the holding.
3. No one is entitled to a holding except by (repeated) applications of 1 and 2.[8]

In strict terms of justice, Nozick proposes this entitlement principle in place of what he calls patterned principles of distribution, such as those based on merit, needs, etc., since it seems to him that any such principles come in the way of transactions on a free-will basis. Thus, if we take seriously the idea of human freedom, we must reject any action that implies despoiling one person of something that belongs to him in order to give it to someone else. A clear example of this situation is taxation, since through taxes someone is deprived of

---

[8] R. Nozick, *Anarchy, State, and Utopia*, p. 151.

what he has earned by the fruit of his labors in order to assign it to others who perhaps have done nothing to deserve it.

Nozick makes use of an example that has become well known to all who discuss patterns of redistribution as a means to obtaining a state of equality, and the relation of equality with liberty: this is the case of Wilt Chamberlain.[9] Let us suppose there is a basket-ball team in which the players are governed by an initial pattern of distribution (D1). We will take for granted that D1 is a pattern of strict equality: they all receive the same salary. One member of the team, Wilt Chamberlain, is its main attraction on account of his superlative style of play.

Assuming that the contracts come up for renewal every year and that the players at this point are free agents, Chamberlain, who is highly sought after, has the option of changing team if the terms of the contract do not satisfy him. As a condition for remaining in the team in which he plays, he proposes to the management a contract with the following clause: every time the team plays at home, 25 cents of the price of each ticket sold will be deposited in a box with his name on it. In one season, a million spectators attend the matches and Wilt Chamberlain thus earns a bonus of $250,000. This sum is well above the average income, and superior even to what other star players earn. We now have D2, a different distribution from the initial one. On the basis of the argument, it is important to point out that with D1 all the players received the same salary and that they all continue to earn this in spite of the special arrangement made with the team's star player. Nozick asks the following question: what arguments can be advanced to show that distribution D2 is unjust? All the spectators choose of their own free will to pay 25 cents to the player, which they might otherwise spend on chocolates, at the movies, or on the subscription to some left-wing review. Besides, if D1 were a just distribution and the players changed voluntarily to D2, is this not likewise a just distribution?

In the example, Nozick demonstrates that if we accept the justice of D2, we must recognize that equality is a separate matter from justice, and that if we value freedom we must reject any kind of patterned principle. In line with these arguments, he thinks that any system regulated by some patterned principle of distribution will impose upon individuals a model of distribution (D1) which will prevent them from making voluntary exchanges and thus limit their exercise of freedom, depriving them of the enjoyment of their freedom to act as they wish. Equality limits the exercise of freedom.

---

[9] Ibid., pp. 160ff.

In Nozick's own words:

> The legitimacy of altering social institutions to achieve greater equality of material condition is, though often assumed, rarely *argued* for. Writers note that in a given country the wealthiest *n* percent of holds more than that percentage of the wealth, and the poorest *n* percent holds less, that to get to the wealth of the top *n* percent from the poorest, one must look at the bottom *p* percent (where *p* is vastly greater than *n*), and so forth. They then proceed immediately to discuss how this might be altered. [...] It cannot merely be *assumed* that equality must be built into any theory of justice. There is a surprising dearth of arguments for equality capable of coming to grips with the considerations that underlie a non-global and nonpatterned conception of justice in holdings.[10]

Nozick examines Bernard Williams' argument in an article entitled "The Idea of Equality", which seeks to deduce, contrary to meritocratic theories, the equality of needs, with the aim of showing that these provide us with a powerful moral weapon against inequality.[11] Williams says:

> Leaving aside preventive medicine, the proper ground of distribution of medical care is ill health; this is a necessary truth. Now in very many societies, while ill health may work as a necessary condition of receiving treatment, it does not work as a sufficient condition, since such treatment costs money, and not all who are ill have the money; hence the possession of sufficient money becomes in fact an additional necessary condition of actually receiving treatment. [...] When we have the situation in which, for instance, wealth is a further necessary condition of the receipt of medical treatment, we can once more apply the notions of equality and inequality: not now in connection with the inequality between the well and the ill, but in connection with the inequality between the rich ill and the poor ill, since we have straightforwardly the situation of those whose needs are the same not receiving the same treatment, though the needs are the ground of the treatment. This is an irrational state of affairs. [...] it is a situation in which reasons are insufficiently *operative*; it is a situation insufficiently controlled by reasons—and hence by reason itself.[12]

Nozick interprets Williams as maintaining that,

> ...if among the different descriptions applying to an activity, there is one that contains an 'internal goal' of the activity, then (it is a necessary truth that) the only proper grounds for the performance of the activity, or its allocating if it

---

[10] Ibid., pp. 232–233.
[11] B. Williams, "The Idea of Equality", pp. 230–249.
[12] Ibid., pp. 240–241 (quoted in Nozick, op. cit., p. 233).

scarce, are connected with the effective achievement of the internal goal. If the activity is done upon other [ground]s, the only proper criterion for distributing the activity is their need for it, if any. Thus it is that Williams says (it is a necessary truth that) the only proper criterion for the distribution of medical care is medical need.[13]

Nozick goes on to comment:

Presumably then, the only proper criterion for the distribution of barbering services is barbering. But why must the internal goal of the activity take precedence over, for example, the person's particular purpose in performing the activity?[14]

As we lack arguments for upholding the position that a person's needs are derived from the internal goal of the activity, we must then conclude that we have no arguments for defending equality. Clearly, as we saw in Chapter III, Nozick believes that the only State which can be justified is a minimal one, and that we lack arguments for proposing a distributive one, since this violates the freedom of the members of a community.

The second thesis against equality states that demands in favor of this are not genuine since they only conceal a feeling of envy. According to the Austrian economist Friedrich A. Hayek,

When we inquire into the justification of these demands, we find that they rest on the discontent that the success of some people often produces in those that are less successful, or to put it bluntly, on envy. The modern tendency to gratify this passion and to disguise it in the respectable garment of social justice is developing into a serious threat to freedom. [...] however human, envy is certainly not one of the sources of discontent that a free society can eliminate. It is probably one of the essential conditions for the preservation of such a society that we do not countenance envy, nor sanction its demands by camouflaging it as social justice, but treat it, in the words of John Stuart Mill, as 'the most anti-social and evil of all passions.[15]

John Rawls has referred to two kinds of envy: general and particular. General envy is generally that "experienced by the least advantaged towards those better situated", who are envied "for the kind of goods and not for the particular objects they possess. The upper

---

[13] R. Nozick, op. cit., pp. 233–234.
[14] Ibid.
[15] F. A. Hayek., *The Constitution of Liberty*, 1978, p. 93.

classes [...] are envied for their greater wealth and opportunity". Particular envy, on the other hand, is "typical of rivalry and competition".[16] Rawls proposes that we make interpersonal comparisons in terms of

> ...the objective primary goods, liberty and opportunity, income and wealth [...]. Then we may think of envy as the propensity to view with hostility the greater good of others even though their being more fortunate than we are does not detract form our advantages. We envy persons whose situation is superior to ours (estimated by some agreed index of goods [...]) and we are willing to deprive them of their greater benefits even if it is necessary to give up something ourselves. When others are aware of our envy, they may become jealous of their better circumstances and anxious to take precautions against the hostile acts to which our envy makes us prone. So understood, envy is collectively disadvantageous: the individual who envies another is prepared to do things that make them both worse off, if only the discrepancy between them is sufficiently reduced. Thus Kant [...] quite properly discusses envy as one of the vices of hating mankind".[17]

Thus, if justice is the social virtue *par excellence*, envy is the greatest vice that the members of a society may experience. Rawls goes on to point out that envy (as opposed to resentment which is an expression of sense of injustice) "is not a moral feeling. No moral principle need be cited in its explanation. It is sufficient to say that the better situation of others catches our attention".[18]

It is necessary to register certain criticisms of the above-mentioned ideas offered in rejection of equality as a goal to be sought after. With regard to Nozick's thesis, there are arguments that demonstrate not only that "patterned principles" do not necessarily violate the liberty of individuals, but also that a power relation might well develop out of Wilt Chamberlain's final position that would affect the freedom of the other players. We might also think that while it is hardly satisfactory to define all activities in terms of their supposed "internal goal", there is no reason why we should not, all the same, view them within their larger social context. A society would be better if levels of inequality in access to goods and services were reduced. G.A. Cohen has questioned the concept of liberty, as

---

[16] J. Rawls, *Theory of Justice*, Harvard, Harvard University Press, 1971, p. 531.

[17] Ibid., p. 532.

[18] Ibid., p. 533.

people like Nozick understand it. It seems to him that liberty understood in this sense is reduced to a mere freedom to buy and sell. For
Cohen it is also possible to think of freedom as something "that
comes in degrees"; for example, "my freedom to do A is, other things
equal, smaller, the greater is the cost to me of doing A". Finally, he
notes that for many people the fact that medical or educational services are provided by the state renders the market simply irrelevant:
"as long as [such services] are obtainable by other means, one should
not exaggerate the gravity of the resulting restrictions on freedom".
To sum up, Cohen thinks that liberty, as "libertarians" understand it,
is "control over *material things*"; therefore, equality may imply limitations on private property, but not on liberty, which is "freedom to
act".[19]

As regards envy, there are arguments in defense of equality that
remove envy from the picture. Rawls, for instance, incorporates the
idea that principles of justice are chosen in a situation of choice in
uncertainty, which guarantees impartiality and eliminates the possibility of envy. Likewise Dworkin has demonstrated the possibility of
eliminating envy from a system of distribution if we achieve a situation in which individuals have equal access to impersonal resources
and that the inequalities that arise from personal resources are compensated for, as we shall see below. Inequalities could be offset by
an insurance system that corresponds to a system of redistribution.
According to Dworkin, it is precisely the absence of envy that would
enable us to arrive at a situation of equality of resources. In this context, envy is not a psychological, but an economic phenomenon. We
might say that someone envies the resources of others when he
would prefer to have those resources rather than his own. Another
argument against envy as a motivation for pursuing claims for equality, lies in the fact that it is conceivable to find ourselves either in a
situation of equality in which yet envy still persists, or in one in of
great inequality where envy is absent; this is due to the fact that, as
we saw in Chapter II, preferences are adaptive and individuals learn
to make do with what they have.

---

[19] See G.A. Cohen, "Illusions about Private Property and Freedom", pp. 225–237.

EQUALITY

The problem of equality is possibly one of the most difficult in political philosophy, since different spheres of social life exist in which equality can be argued about, and there are also different ways of conceiving of it. This will be the subject of the following section.

As Thomas Nagel observes, contemporary political debate has to address four different kinds of equality: political, legal, social and economic. "Political equality is not guaranteed by guaranteeing each adult one vote and the right to hold public office. Legal equality is not guaranteed by granting everyone the right to a jury trial, the right to bring suit for injuries, and the right to counsel. Social equality is not produced by the abolition of titles and official barriers to class mobility",[20] nor by the abolition of color bars or religious discrimination for that matter. While political institutions can guarantee a bottom-line social status for everyone, differences in wages and incomes can lead to considerable inequalities when it comes to action on political, legal and social spheres. The effects of economic inequality can be easily seen in the political sphere, for instance. People in a state of extreme poverty often find it difficult to express their political preferences by voting. This may be due to their homes being in remote areas at a great distance from the nearest polling station. On the other hand, the vote of the poor is often induced; even programs designed to alleviate poverty may be utilized for purposes of clientelism. With regard to legal inequality, it has also been observed that access to legal assistance inevitably varies in accordance with people's economic situations. Social inequality is directly related to economic inequality, since while Article One of the Mexican Constitution states formally that: "In Mexico every individual shall enjoy the guarantees laid down in this Constitution, which shall be neither restricted nor suspended, except in the cases and subject to the conditions established herein", the paths for fulfillment of this prescription are directly related to the economic situation of each citizen. For example, in Mexico, approximately 10 million individuals do not have a birth certificate, a phenomenon directly related to poverty. The poor are generally those "excluded" from political, legal and social arrangements.[21]

---

[20] Thomas Nagel, "Equality", p. 106.

[21] In this respect, see P. Dieterlen, "Democracia, pobreza y exclusión", pp. 121–174.

One way of dealing with the problem of equality is to establish a distinction between horizontal and vertical equality; this means that, in terms of the former, we must treat equals as equals, and in terms of the latter, unequals as unequals. The problem with this way of approaching equality is that from time to time we shall need a criterion that is not always clear for detecting equalities and inequalities relevant for the purposes of distribution. Due to the lack of agreement that frequently manifests itself regarding what is relevant for distribution, contemporary discussion has tended to center on *what* is to be distributed.

1) Equality as distribution of an equalisandum

When dealing with equality it is important to identify what is often referred to as an *equalisandum*. A proposition which comprises an *equalisandum* must specify what is to be made equal, in other words what it is that individuals must be equal in.[22]

A good principle for approaching the problem of equality from the point of view of the *equalisandum* is to be found in Amartya Sen's article "Equality of What? In this work Sen examines several answers to the question, among which we find the equality of what, in Chapter II, we called criteria of distribution.

One of the *equalisanda* most discussed is that of well-being, understood as the satisfaction of preferences. The theory of equality of well-being holds that society should render the well-being of all people equal or contribute in an egalitarian manner so that all its members achieve their well-being and all individuals should be subjects of equality. From this point of view, men and women should obtain the things on which their interests focus. If individuals are equally important, the State must implement policies that enable their preferences to be equally satisfied. This theory has been widely criticized for three reasons which I shall examine below. The first is the lack of a criterion regarding which kinds of preferences must count in a distribution and which are to be left aside. Individuals have a diversity of preferences; the theory would, however, commit us to allocating more resources to people with more emphatic preferences, or to ego-

---

[22] For a discussion of different categories of *equalisanda,* see G.A. Cohen, "On the Currency of Egalitarian Justice".

ists rather than to charitable persons. The second is that at times, in order to equalize society's preferences it would be necessary to lower the level of satisfaction of each and all; we could even go as far as to maintain that in some cases of egalitarian satisfaction of preferences it is required that the exercise of certain rights be limited. The third reason is that no boundary is set between preferences and needs, nor between the efforts (or lack of efforts) by individuals to contribute to society. The problem with theories of equality of well-being lies in the fact that they are obliged to take into account the expensive tastes of one person that affect the satisfaction of the preferences of other members of society.[23] On the other hand it is important to remember that preferences tend to adapt themselves to the range of available possibilities, and this presents serious problems for the equality of well-being. In Jon Elster's words, we can even find cases in which wishes cause beliefs to alter, in other words, cases of "sour grapes".

Equalisanda—like the primary goods, needs, capacities and resources—have arisen in response to the problems associated with the notion of equality of well-being. Nonetheless, when we examine the said criteria of distribution, we find certain problems. For, instance, primary goods are set somehow apart from individuals and do not attend to the particularities of persons and their cultural environment. On the other hand, we have seen that capacities, above all the basic ones, are easily reduced to needs, and we also saw that it is difficult to implement a public policy based on such capacities. As for needs, we find (while these constitute the basis of any policy of equality) that at times it is difficult to establish a criterion for distinguishing them. Despite this, it is reasonable to state that certain basic needs exist that correspond to our intuitions regarding what is urgent for ensuring that a life is a "human" life. The problem of needs is that it can leave aside an important element for establishing conditions of equality, which is choice. As we saw in the above-mentioned chapter, we need a mixed criterion, in other words one which encompasses both an objective element such as needs and a subjective one such as choices.

---

[23] See E. Rakowski, *Equal Justice*, pp. 39–41. A detailed critique of the theories of equality of well-being is to be found in R. Dworkin, "Equality of Welfare", 1981.

An indispensable distinction for approaching the problem of equality is that which exists between inequalities that depend on individuals' choices and those which do not. Ronald Dworkin takes this distinction into account and suggests an approach based on equality of resources. Its starting point is the difference that exists between the bad luck ("option luck") which comes about as a result of the choices made by individuals, and "brute luck", which originates in situations that go beyond the framework of choice. For example a person may be worse off than another because he placed all his hopes in a bad investment or because he was born blind.[24]

To understand the distinction Dworkin asks us to consider an imaginary story. Let us suppose that a ship is wrecked on an island possessing a wide variety of resources. It ought to be perfectly possible to distribute these resources in an egalitarian manner by means of the following procedure: all the available resources are divided up by auctioned after allotting to each person on the island the same amount of money or vouchers for purchase. We can thus be sure that the distribution of goods will pass what Dworkin calls the "envy test":[25] everyone was free to choose what resources to buy, and everyone must therefore be satisfied with his or her choice. Once the auction is over, people can set about their work and engage in such exchanges as suit them and make such investments as they wish. All the persons who arrived on the island have decided in advance which resources they wished to possess, distribution was egalitarian, even though each person's resources will be different.

This situation would remain true if we could assume that individuals are themselves equal in all aspects. In this context, however, it is important to remember that people possess two kinds of resources: personal and impersonal resources. The former are individuals' own untransferable resource: their physical and mental capacities, their talents and their health; such resources are important for each person to be able to carry out her projects and her goals. Impersonal resources, on the other hand, are part of an individual's environment and can be possessed and transferred. This category includes money, land, raw materials, real estate and legal rights. The pertinence of this distinction is that the auction can only take place in relation with impersonal resources. The problem may then arise that, while the initially egalitarian purchase of impersonal resources may pass the envy test, personal resources may generate situations of inequality. Once the auction is over, people will begin to produce and to exchange voluntarily; their talents, abilities and skills will, however, destroy the initial equality of impersonal resources. In this situation what Dworkin calls "brute luck" also comes into play, in other words the luck that is manifested in certain risks that it is not

---

[24] See Ronald Dworkin, "What is Equality? Part 2. Equality of Resources", p. 293.
[25] The distribution satisfies the "envy test" when no immigrant "would prefer someone else's bundle of resources to his own bundle", op. cit. p. 285.

possible to anticipate, and that people are not willing to run. Finally, his proposal of equality consists in implementing compensatory insurance policies for people who find themselves in a situation of inequality due to the brute ill luck that might arise from their personal resources. Returning to the island, it is easy to imagine that we could add to the conditions of the auction certain insurance policies that might offer protection against a large variety of risks such as accidents, sickness or very low wages. Individuals could freely do without certain commodities and in their place buy those insurance policies that would enable them to mitigate the effects of brute bad luck.

Dworkin notes that, in the real world, systems of taxes and redistribution of income exist for the purposes of providing opportunities of employment, medical attention, and educational resources, such as is manifested in the hypothetical market. Redistributive taxes would reduce the inequality of resources, both personal and impersonal.

A crucial element that Dworkin mentions is that of the manifestation of preferences that individuals might make in this imaginary auction. In theories of equality, preference is important. When we speak of equality, it is necessary to take into account both factors that depend on the choice of individuals and those that are foreign to their choice.

Dworkin tries to reconcile freedom with equality when he affirms that liberals accept two principles:

> The first requires that people have, at any point in their lives, different amounts of wealth insofar as the genuine choices they have made have been more or less expensive or beneficial to the community, measured by what other people want for their lives. The market seems indispensable to this principle. The second requires that people not have different amounts of wealth just because they have different inherent capacities to produce what others want, or are differently favored by chance. This means that market allocations must be corrected in order to bring some people closer to the share of resources they would have had but for these various differences of initial advantage, luck and inherent capacity.[26]

Despite the influence of Dworkin's thought on equality, some authors believe that a theory of equality needs to give more weight to the circumstances in which people find themselves, since these in one way or another determine individuals' possibilities when it comes to transforming their personal resources into well-being. Dworkin has also been criticized for failing to consider the fact that people are generally responsible for the formation of their preferences. G. A. Cohen, for example, thinks that the important difference in a theory of equality is the difference between responsibility and

---

[26] Ronald Dworkin, "Why Liberals Should Care about Equality", p. 207.

bad luck, rather than that between resources and preferences, since a theory of equality can scarcely differentiate between one's responsibility for having expensive tastes and one's responsibility for wasting valuable resources.[27]

Some philosophers who defend equality prefer not to speak in terms of some *equalisandum* or another, but in terms of the somewhat more abstract notion of opportunities.[28]

2) Equality of opportunities

One way of approaching the problem of equality is to treat it as equality of opportunities, as Rawls explains in the second principle of justice. Rather than concentrating on the *equalisandum* themselves, equality of opportunities stresses the role played by the *equalisanda* in offering individuals an enhanced possibility of competing for certain positions in society. Thus Rawls tells us that the second principle of justice, which he calls the "difference principle", gives a certain value to measures for compensation, and he states that undeserved inequalities have to be compensated for. The principle maintains that with the aim of treating all individuals equally and providing an authentic equality of opportunities, society will have to give greater attention, on the one hand, to those who have less natural gifts and, on the other, to those who have been born in socially less favorable positions. His idea consists in compensating for contingent disadvantages in the direction of equality. The difference principle allocates resources in such a way as to improve the long-term expectations of the least favored.[29] Nevertheless, for Rawls, a way of compensating the least well off is by redistributing primary goods, which, as we have already seen, represent certain problems, such as their heterogeneity. Some critics have noted the insensitivity of Rawls's theory both to the particular gifts of individuals, and to their disabilities: his principles might, for example, lead us to the conclusion that "a person with a relatively high income, but with severe physical disabilities, would [...] would be better off than [a

---

[27] See G.A. Cohen, "Currency of Egalitarian Justice", p. 924.

[28] A very detailed discussion on critiques of Rawls, Dworkin and Sen can be found in Roberto Gargarella's book, *Las teorías de la justicia después de Rawls*, pp. 69–85.

[29] See John Rawls, *Theory of Justice*, 1971, pp. 100ff.

poorer but physically healthy person], even though his higher income might be insufficient" to compensate for his disadvantages. It has also been observed that Rawls's theory is not sufficiently sensitive to personal ambition, since part of the ambitious person's additional resources will necessarily have to be distributed to those who are less well off because they have, through indolence, failed to develop their talents to the full.[30]

Perhaps one of the most interesting treatments of equality of opportunities is to be found in the work of John Roemer.[31] Roemer begins by mentioning two approaches to equality of opportunity that, he says, "prevalent today in Western democracies". The first is what is referred to as "leveling the playing field"—by, for example, making sure children from disadvantaged backgrounds are given the necessary compensatory education to make them able to compete for jobs with those from more advantaged homes. The second, "the non-discrimination principle", holds that all competitors for access to jobs who possess the appropriate qualities to perform the duties entailed must be eligible, irrespective of such irrelevant characteristics as race, sex or the social standing of their family. Roemer views the principle of non-discrimination "as deriving from a particular interpretation of the level-the-playing-field principle" since by ruling out discrimination on the basis of such irrelevant characteristics the playing field is indeed to that degree leveled.[32]

According to Roemer, any theorist who defends equality of opportunities will "hold the individual accountable for the achievement of the advantage" they are able to acquire. These may be "a level of educational achievement, health, employment status, income, or the economist's utility or welfare. Thus there is in the notion of equality of opportunity a 'before' and an 'after'": *before* in the sense that it is before the start of the competition that the playing field has to be leveled in order to reduce initial inequalities as far as possible. Once this has been done, individuals "are on their own".[33]

Roemer describes his aim as pluralist in two senses: the first in offering a methodology "consonant with any of a spectrum of views on

---

[30] See R. Gargarella, op. cit., p. 72.

[31] See J. Roemer, *Equality of Opportunity*.

[32] Op. cit., p. 1.

[33] Ibid., p. 2.

individual accountability"; the second in the possibility of accommodating it to different theories of distributive justice. Thus the purpose of an equal opportunities policy is, above all, to level the playing field, in other words to ensure that all sectors of the population have the same possibility of attaining the desired advantages. Now, in order to level the field of play, we must first distinguish between those differential circumstances inherent to individuals and those for which they cannot be held accountable, but may well affect their possibilities to compete for certain positions. For example, education is universally recognized as a means for having access to certain positions; equality of opportunities might seem to be achieved by ensuring that the same quantity of educational resources be given to all individuals. Nevertheless, guaranteeing equal per capita financing for education is not sufficient to obtain educational achievements, "since different children are able to use educational resources [...] with different degrees of effectiveness or efficiency".[34]

The important thing is to design educational inputs in such a way as to compensate for those differences in the "ability to process educational resources" that are determined by "circumstances beyond a child's control", since it is these educational resources, once transformed into educational achievement, that later will manifest themselves as competitive skills. To do this we must first distinguish between such circumstances and the child's "acts of autonomous volition and effort" since there is no justification for attempting to level the latter. The "ability" to effect the above-mentioned transformation is defined in terms of what the child is able to do "by virtue of the influence of circumstances beyond her control, which [...] include her genes, her family background, her culture, and more generally, her social milieu".[35]

Once the playing field has been leveled, and those inequalities have been attended to that did not depend on the "freely chosen effort" of individuals, we shall pass on to the *afterwards* of distribution, in other words to observe the results of the effort made by individuals to transform resources in elements that offer them possibilities to enter into competition for the jobs they wish to occupy.

---

[34] Ibid., p. 6.
[35] Ibid., p. 6.

Roemer proposes the establishment of a sort of grid for classifying children into a finite number of *types* according to their circumstances. For instance, individuals who are in a state of extreme poverty as characterized by one or another of the criteria mentioned in Chapter I might well fall into one particular social *type*. An equal opportunities policy has first to raise the level of the playing field in respect of each social *type* by the amount needed to bring it up to the level of the more advantaged groups. Once their position has been leveled one can observe the efforts they make and the responsibility they exercise to transform their resources and thus to be able to compete in conditions of equality. If, for instance, the effort and moral responsibility of a person, within a particular *type*, is greater, he or she must receive more resources in order to have more possibilities to enter into competition.[36] On the other hand, differentiating between effort or responsibility on the one hand and circumstances on the other enables us to compare achievements between persons who find themselves in different *types* and thus to allocate resources in the most egalitarian manner. If the achievements obtained by two citizens belonging to the same *type* vary, it can be assumed that this is because their efforts varied. We can speak of moral responsibility, on the other hand to the degree that (in Thomas Scanlon's words)

> ...what we do be importantly dependent on our process of critical reflection, that that process itself be sensitive to reasons, and that later stages of the process be importantly dependent on conclusions reached at earlier stages. But there is no reason, as far as I can see, to require that this process this process itself not be a causal product of antecedent events and conditions.[37]

Roemer acknowledges a certain vagueness in the term *opportunity* since it is "not a school or a plate of nourishing food or a warm abode, but is, rather, a capacity which is brought into being by properly using that school, food, and hearth".[38] He takes up a concept expressed by G.H. Cohen, for whom an opportunity is an "access to advantage". In Cohen's own words,

> ...equality of access to advantage is motivated by the idea that differential advantage is unjust, save where it reflects differences in genuine choice (or, more or

---

[36] Ibid., p. 7.
[37] Cited by J. Roemer, ibid., p. 17.
[38] Cf. ibid., p. 24.

less, capability) on the part of relevant agents; but it is not genuine choice as such (or capability) which the view proposes to equalize. The idea motivating equality of access to advantage does not even imply that there actually is such a thing as genuine choice. Instead, it implies that if there is no such thing—because, for example, 'hard determinism' is true—then all differential advantage is unjust.[39]

A similar idea has been expressed by Julian LeGrand[40] as follows: it is possible to define the factors that do not depend on an individual's control, as his *constraints*. We can define the group of possibilities limited by an individual's constraints as his *choice set*. A situation is then "*equitable if it is the outcome of individuals choosing over equal choice sets*". The problem that arises in the cases of individuals in a state of poverty is that their possibilities are very restricted and are not subject to their control.

The importance of these approaches is that they address, as objective factors, conditions that do not depend on individuals, such as, for instance, the place where they were born and their real possibilities to take decisions. But they also regard as indispensable their capacity to choose particular life plans. Any egalitarian policy of distributive justice must consider both aspects.

In conclusion, it can noted that when we speak of a principle of equality that does not enter into conflict with freedom, we need to take into account both those circumstances that are foreign to people's choices and the choices they are free to make. Typifying individuals according to a schema like that suggested by Roemer commits us to the raising of their standard of living. In cases of extreme poverty, leveling the field of play for them implies attending to their basic needs. Once these are satisfied it is possible to observe the choices people make in order to transform, for instance, the satisfaction of needs into job possibilities. However, the more uneven the "playing field", the more institutional policies need to be strengthened, without ceasing to take into account individuals' responsibility and the efforts they make.

There is no doubt that the problem of equality is one of the most complex in political philosophy. As we have already seen, there are many ways of approaching it, such as vertical and horizontal equality, equality of *equalisanda*, and as equality of opportunities. An-

---

[39] G.A. Cohen, "Equality of What? On Welfare, Goods and Capabilities", p. 28.
[40] See J. Le Grand, "Equity as an Economic Objective", p. 190.

other very serious problem that arises when we focus on equality is the question of the motivations of individuals to aspire to an egalitarian society. We saw earlier on that the critics of equality think that the only motivation that exists for seeking equality is envy. Nonetheless, while rejecting this idea, we have to offer an explanation of a possible motivation for aiming at a more egalitarian society.

IS THERE ANY REASON FOR SEEKING EQUALITY?

This question is pertinent because it seems that inequality is often seen as a natural state of affairs, or as merely a result of good luck. Many of us are so accustomed to it that it appears to us a social fact that it is difficult to imagine being changed. A number of philosophers and economists think, however, that such affirmations are at best founded on error and in the worst of cases reflect a narrowing down of human motivations in response to strictly personal preferences. They affirm that our motivations are in fact multiple and that among these is concern for others. Of course, there is no reason why we cannot act under the motivation of economic utility and at the same time wish for equality as a means of obtaining greater security, but the important thing is to discover within ourselves those motivations that allow us to approach an egalitarian ideal. We do not have to be saints, or to imagine that we must always be carrying out actions that go beyond the call of duty. We may simply take for granted that human beings are *naturally* concerned about each other. To believe anything else would be to think of ourselves, in Sen's words, as "rational fools".

There are several answers to the question regarding motivation and almost all of them refer to the capacity of human beings for having personal preferences, but also non-personal preferences among which figures our concern for others. As we saw in Chapter III in connection with obligations, an important motivation is altruism, which consists in considering the needs of others from a non-personal point of view. This means that, as Nagel observes, we can feel a concern for others, as long as the conviction exists that others are concerned about us. If we consider that the lives of all people are equally valuable, relieving the urgent needs of others constitutes a reason for combating inequality.

Sen, on the other hand, thinks that we need to distinguish two motivations that help explain our altruistic behavior towards others: these are sympathy and what he refers to as "commitment".[41] "The former corresponds to the case in which the concern for others directly affects one's own welfare"; if you actually feel bad when you are aware of something horrible happening to others, what you are experiencing is sympathy. Commitment, on the other hand, refers to one's readiness to make choices on the basis of judgments concerning the welfare of others, whether or not this has a direct effect on one's own welfare (we can be sure we are witnessing a case of commitment, when a person acts in a way that is actually likely to "yield a lower level of personal welfare to him than an alternative that is already available to him").[42] Another important motivation is generated when we think of society as the manifestation of a great social pact or contract, in which we commit ourselves, as Rawls has shown, to a principle of respect for the liberty and equality of all. If we want the pact to be honored we must avoid two situations: the first of these would be to allow any citizen to remain outside the pact: we can call this the condition of inclusion; the second would be a weakening of the pact, as a result of such inequalities as might arise through the overwhelming success of certain individuals through the exercise of their personal capacities or skills. We must be in a position constantly to renew the initial situation of equality: we can call this the condition of rectification. This means that we cannot afford to let the "playing field", to use Roemer's term once again, to become too tilted against those who set out from a less advantaged position.

Another type of motivation is that described by Villoro: the desire to make dreams come true, or that which arises in us when we imagine a more perfect situation than that which actually exists, and which compels us to seek to attain it. This means that, if we are capable of conceiving a less unequal society, we will surely seek the means to arrive at it.

While attaining a less unequal state without detriment to freedom is a very demanding task, it is possible to suggest the implementation of particularized egalitarian policies. This can be done by focusing on the social *types* that need most attention. Since the present work

---

[41] See "Rational Fools", pp. 95 ff.
[42] Ibid., p. 95.

has been concerned with the study of poverty, the following section will examine an example of how one can begin to combat the inequality of those who belong to the *type* of the extreme poor, and within this general type, that of women, who in most countries with high levels of poverty form an even more deprived *subtype*.

PROGRESA AND THE EQUALITY OF WOMEN

One of the particular aims of PROGRESA has been to combat the inequality existing between men and women. This inequality manifests itself in two ways: the first that, within poor families, women receive a less favorable distribution of goods; the second that families in which women are heads of households are generally the worst-off of all. As José Gómez de León and Susan Parker point out:

The poverty of female heads of households has become a noteworthy phenomenon at the world level: the so-called 'feminization of poverty'. In many countries evidence has been found that households headed by women have a greater likelihood of being poor than those with a male head of household. The greater degree of poverty has been explained in terms of several reasons, such as the absence of a partner (since women must take care of both family income and domestic chores). Also, women generally command lower incomes in the labor market, whether because of discrimination or because they have less experience or education; all these factors impede their efforts to maintain their families.[43]

PROGRESA implemented two measures aimed at achieving a reduction in inequality between men and women: first, that economic support is given to the housewives; secondly, that the amount of money given in educational grants for girls is greater than that for boys. Now, as we have seen, there are countless divergent theses regarding the key factors to be taken into account when discussing equality: in other words, exactly what it is that needs to be equalized. As has already been mentioned, the term "equality" begins to have sense as a constitutional expression, in other words as one based on a relationship with law. All citizens, both men and women, ought to have the same rights and obligations. However, as we have already seen, students of the problem of equality have emphasized that en-

---

[43] José Gómez de Léon and Susan Parker. "Bienestar y jefatura femenina en los hogares mexicanos", p. 11.

suring equality before the law means little if economic equality is not taken into account. This has an important impact on the demands of constitutional equality. One of the formulas that comes closest to the egalitarian ideal states that a policy must treat equals as equals and unequals as unequals. The importance of this approach lies in the fact that it is possible to detect inequalities with the aim of effecting a redistribution. For this reason it makes sense to implement social polices that attend to the relevant differences. In the case of the implementation of PROGRESA, as was mentioned in Chapter II, three criteria of distribution were mentioned—needs, preferences and capacities; we could also have recourse to a notion of equality that refers both to horizontal and vertical equality. The latter takes us back to the criterion that enables us to treat unequals unequally, as long as we possess a sure means for detecting the relevant differences. In the case of PROGRESA a relevant difference is that of gender.

With the problem of equality as our background, we can detect the existence of at least three arguments for a social policy that seeks to influence the situation of inequality faced by women. The first contemplates the importance of support to the women in recognition of the situation of exclusion and marginalization they have faced historically and culturally. In this way it seeks to reduce gender inequality. This argument is strictly compensatory. A social policy has the obligation to reduce inequality on account of having allowed it in the past. In this sense, to allow relates to the notion of "letting something happen", in other words with the idea of failing to remove an obstacle that was preventing a series of events from taking place. The obstacles may be physical, cultural, social and historical. This argument is based on a situation of injustices committed in the past. This thesis is contrary to that of Jon Elster, who maintains that the mechanisms of distribution must be "presentist", in other words they should apply to injustices that are taking place exclusively in the present.[44]

The second argument is related to equality of opportunities, in other words to the benefit the improvement of the situation of women will cause in families and in society in general. For instance, as is well known, when the level of education of mothers rises, the number of children they have tends to descend, thus enabling social

---

[44] See J. Elster., *Local Justice*, p. 195.

attention to be improved. Schooling provides women with instruments for deciding freely and consciously regarding their right to reproduction. This argument is based on the results that will be achieved if the situation of inequality currently faced by women is improved. An essential factor for reducing the inequality between men and women, for example, is education. This is a fundamental factor for individuals to enter fully into the social and economic life of the country. Besides, being a constitutional right, education is a basic need that contributes to the development of the capacities required for carrying out well remunerated productive activities. The appropriate term for designating such policies, as we have already seen, is that of equality of opportunities. For instance, a good education influences the development of families, and good health facilitates better performance at work. Education has a substantial impact on reducing the inequality of women, since it brings them access to the information and knowledge necessary to take advantage of the resources and services available to them, as well as to take better care of their health and that of their families. Education provides two tools that enable women to escape from their situation of marginalization: the first is knowledge, which increases their opportunities in life; the second is the learning techniques that they may come to use in a variety of life situations. Perhaps one of the most important characteristics of education is that it help preventing people to rid their destinies of the determining effect of the circumstances that surround them, in other words to reduce their subjection to factors beyond their control; by doing so, they considerably increase their possibilities of choice. The more possibilities a woman has—via knowledge—to set herself at a distance from her immediate situation, the more opportunities she will have to change it. By opening more paths for personal improvement, education makes possible the exercise of freedom and tends to reduce the inequalities of gender. On the other hand, to be beneficiaries of PROGRESA, women have to accept certain responsibilities, such as attending the talks related to preventive health care, going to the health clinics on a regular basis, and making sure their children attend school. Now, one problem that has been detected in PROGRESA is that the demand for health services and school enrollment has increased. This has resulted in the availability of doctors and schools becoming insufficient. For this reason, following Roemer, we might think that it is necessary to level the "playing field" for the benefit of one *type* in particular, in this case that of the rural teachers and the doctors who staff these clinics. Often the particular circumstances of the place where schools are located make their work difficult and constitute a block on their responsibility and their efforts.

The third, and most important, argument refers to the First and Fourth Articles of the Constitution. The First Article states that: "In Mexico, every individual shall enjoy the guarantees granted in this Constitution, which may not be suspended, except in the cases and under the conditions established herein". Article 4, on the other hand, sets forth that: "Men and women are equal before the law. The law shall protect the organization and development of the family". It is worth mentioning the essential nature of both negative and positive rights for the purposes of fulfilling the stipulations of Article 4 of the Constitution. The former have to do with the obligation of the State and other citizens not to inhibit the rights of women; this includes ensuring violence against them is punished, but also avoiding other forms of coercion. Positive rights involve all those actions which give people who lack them the necessary means for developing certain capacities. It is not only a matter of removing obstacles to freedom of expression, but also of ensuring that a policy that attends to the needs of women should foster their capacity to exercise the said freedom.

The two former arguments for intervention to improve the situation of women—that of compensation by means of special support for a pasta and present of exclusion and marginalization, and the fact that attending to the situation of women will increase equality of opportunities for the community at large—take on an even greater significance to the degree that such action strengthens the equality of the sexes that is enshrined in the Constitution.

Every social policy that lays priority on attention to women must implement mechanisms that enable their relevant differences to be detected and, on that basis, introduce such laws as may be necessary for their state of inequality to be mitigated. To be "equal" means being able to being able to develop one's capabilities and modes of functioning, and being treated with the same consideration and the same respect as men. To achieve this government and society must provide the necessary means for the development of autonomy and the capacity to choose.

In conclusion, I should like to stress that liberty and equality are not conflicting principles, but rather complementary ones. The exercise of freedom implies that all claims should be listened to, and if possible attended to. As more possibilities for exercising freedom come into existence, we shall have more guarantees that the demands arising from unsatisfied needs will be attended to. Perhaps, as thinkers such as G.A. Cohen and Amartya Sen have pointed out, it would be a good thing to review our system of property rights. It is also necessary to distance ourselves from that idea of liberty that reduces it to the freedom of market transactions. Finally, we should remember that a lessening of inequality in any society will contribute to a strengthening of basic liberties. Both are political ideals that we must not abandon.

CONCLUSIONS

That the problem of poverty merits attention from different fields of knowledge can hardly be doubted. Economics has contributed importantly to the building up of indexes which enable us to identify families undergoing conditions of extreme poverty, to providing indicators that, in the best of cases, have been applied to implement public policies aimed at combating this condition. Other branches of the social sciences, such as anthropology and sociology, have set about studying the characteristics and behavior patterns of people who are suffering that kind of situation as well as the further problems caused by poverty.

Philosophy has not remained behind. Practically the entirety of the ethical tradition, at least in the West, has proposed standards or modes of behavior enabling men and women to be free and not to act under pressure from causes foreign to what has traditionally been called "their will". It has also included as an essential element of good conduct, the rationality of human beings, in other words their capacity to propose for themselves their own life plans and choose the means they consider to be most appropriate to achieve them. These conditions can hardly be met in the case of human beings who are occupied day after day in their mere struggle for survival.

For such reasons, it seems necessary to discuss the subject of human dignity. Poverty prevents human beings from acting with autonomy since it locks them into what we have called its "vicious circles". If in the society we live in today there are individuals who are unable to transcend their dependence on others, or on their environments, we can scarcely claim to have reached, as citizens, an ethically acceptable level. As an article describing the aims of PROGRESA affirms:

> Poverty is a condition that prevents the basic needs of individuals from being satisfied and their full participation in society from being realized. Poverty injures individuals not only because of the material deprivation it implies, but because it limits the possibilities for developing their basic human capacities.[1]

---

[1] J. Gómez de Léon *et al*, "El Programa de Educación, Salud y Alimentación: orientaciones y componentes", p. 5.

Likewise, ethics is committed to a number of different ways of conceiving of human beings. For example, if we consider human needs to be satisfied with resources that merely ensure their staying alive, this will surely influence the way we go about combating poverty. If, on the other hand, we believe that the list of those things that the satisfaction of human needs requires a much more extensive range of goods, our approach will be of a more complex and richer nature. For those of us who live in countries where a large proportion of the population lives in extreme poverty, the subject of needs is unavoidable. While arguments about the subject are often difficult and lacking in precision, we must find the way to "set a line" and perhaps to speak of a package of needs that must be satisfied, regardless of the different ways in which this may be done and the specificity of each culture.

Nonetheless, I am aware that the concept of need can generate a passive concept of human beings. It has, therefore, been my interest to rescue the notion of preference. A criterion of distribution must find a way to attend to the satisfaction of needs while also allowing people to exercise their preferences. It seems to me that this idea to some degree coincides with Amartya Sen's idea of capabilities. I understand preference as the way in which people decide to carry on their lives; nobody can exercise such a preference does not enjoy conditions of basic autonomy. In a country with a high rate of poverty, we cannot avoid taking into account basic needs: at least those for food, health and basic education. This book took as one of its starting points the existence of basic needs common to all mankind; what may vary is perhaps the ways in which such needs are satisfied. This approach commits us accepting certain cultural differences, without leaving out of the picture needs as a source of imperatives that must be attended to. We also recognize, however, that a policy of attention to poverty must enable people to take decisions regarding the way in which the resources provided by support programs are to be used. Those responsible for implementing public policies must be aware that the beneficiaries are autonomous persons with the capacity for free choice. As long as they do so they will avoid the paternalism that often accompanies campaigns to fight poverty.

As far as political philosophy is concerned, a wide-ranging discussion is taking place at present on the subject of welfare or social rights. The recognition of such rights constitutes an incentive for the distribution goods and services as provided for by national constitutions or the legal frameworks of different countries. Nevertheless, the overwhelming scarcity affecting those countries with a high index of poverty prevents these rights from being completely satisfied. It seems to me that in a country like Mexico there are two ways to try to get around this problem. The first consists in seeking ways to ensure that social rights such as the right to education and medical attention cease to be mere programmatic norms and become rights "in a strong sense", in other words enforceable rights. For this purpose it is necessary to have a legal system accessible to those who most need it. We then have to commit ourselves to an ongoing discussion of the matter and to watch over the fulfillment of public policies. For example, as Nora Lustig mentions: "It is extremely important that the community interested in, and committed to, combating poverty in Mexico should demand that social programs like PROGRESA are not affected by budget cuts".[2] The other way, perhaps more demanding, would consist in being aware that, as citizens, we have obligations towards those people involved in a mere struggle for survival, whose conditions prevent them from developing any kind of life plan.

At present a great debate is going on between the so-called liberal and the communitarian theories. While this was not the subject of this book, I could hardly avoid addressing the question of social norms; this is due to the plurality of communities existing in Mexico. What I have argued is that, while it cannot be denied that the methods most used for measuring poverty are based on the concept of utility, it is appropriate to take into account the fact that individuals often behave in response to norms, rather than the maximization of utility. In the case of poor communities, these norms are mainly of a social nature. Public policies must take them into account if programs are to have the greatest possible effect. We must, nevertheless, reject those norms that distance us from the democratic ideals of equality and liberty.

The subject of equality is intimately connected with the problem of poverty: it thus seemed appropriate to consider some of the theo-

---

[2] Nora Lustig, "Reflexiones sobre las características del Programa PROGRESA", in *Alivio a la pobreza. Análisis del Programa de Educación, Salud y Alimentación dentro de la política social*, Memoria del Seminario, CIESAS, PROGRESA, 1998, p. 128.

ries that have been developed in this field. Those authors who set forth criteria for distribution believe that their application brings us closer to an egalitarian society. Perhaps one of the most interesting problems in political philosophy is the compatibility that must exist between basic liberties and those principles that enable us to approach a more egalitarian society; equality and liberty are two political ideals that complement each other. A theory of equality must take basic needs into account in order to raise people's standards of living; once this has been achieved, resources can be distributed in accordance with the responsibility and effort shown by those benefiting from programs. All this can be demanded once people's basic needs are really satisfied, particularly when we are faced with conditions of extreme poverty.

Finally, this book has addressed the way in which philosophical theories and concepts are applied in a Program designed to combat extreme poverty. My aim was to demonstrate that discussions in philosophy have a field of application, in other words they are not mere abstract discussions separate from reality. I hope this purpose has been fulfilled.

REFERENCES

Almond, Brenda, and Donald Hill (eds.), *Applied Philosophy. Moral and Metaphysics in Contemporary Debate*, Routledge, London/New York, 1991.

Aristotle, *The Ethics* (*Nichomachean Ethics*), tr. J.A.K. Thomson, Penguin Classics, Harmondsworth, 1953.

Arrow, Kenneth, *Social Choice and Individual Values*, Yale University Press, New Haven, 1963.

Atkinson, A.B., "Promise and Performance: Why We Need an Official Poverty Report", in Paul Barker (ed.), *Living as Equals*, Oxford University Press, Oxford, 1996, pp. 123–141.

Barry, Brian, *Theories of Justice*, vol. I, Berkeley, University of California Press, 1989.

Berlin, Isaiah, "Two Concepts of Liberty", in A. Quinton (ed.), *Political Philosophy*, pp. 141–152.

Boltvinik, Julio, "Conceptos y medidas de la pobreza", in J. Boltvinik and E. Hernández Laos, *Pobreza y distribución del ingreso en México*, pp. 30–80.

———, "El conocimiento de la pobreza en México", in J. Boltvinik and E. Hernández Laos, *Pobreza y distribución del ingreso en México*, pp. 81–118.

———, "Métodos de medición de la pobreza. Conceptos y tipología", *Socialis, Revista Latinoamericana de Política Social*, no. 1, October 1999, pp. 35–74.

———, "Métodos de medición de la pobreza. Una evaluación crítica", *Socialis: Revista Latinoamericana de Política Social*, no. 2, May, 2000, pp. 83–123.

———, "Opciones metodológicas para medir la pobreza en México", *Comercio Exterior*, vol. 51, no. 10, México, October 2001, pp. 869–878.

Boltvinik, Julio, and Enrique Hernández Laos, *Pobreza y distribución del ingreso en México*, Siglo XXI, México, 1999.

Brock, Dan, "Quality of Life Measures in Health Care and Medical Ethics", in M. Nussbaum and A. Sen (eds.), *The Quality of Life*, pp. 135–178.

Brock, Gillian (ed.), *Necessary Goods. Our Responsibilities to Meet Others' Needs*, Rowman and Littlefield, Oxford/New York, 1998.

Carbonell, Miguel, Juan Antonio Cruz Parcero and Rodolfo Vázquez (eds.), *Derechos sociales y derechos de las minorías*, Instituto de Investigaciones Jurídicas-UNAM, Mexico City, 2000.

Charlesworth, Max, *Bioethics in a Liberal Society*, Cambridge University Press, Cambridge, 1993.

Cohen, G.A., "Equality of What? On Welfare, Goods and Capabilities", in M. Nussbaum and A. Sen (eds.), *The Quality of Life*, pp. 9–30.

———, "Illusions About Private Property and Freedom", in J. Mepham and D. Rubens (eds.), *Issues in Marxist Philosophy*, vol. IV, Harvester Press, Brighton, 1981, pp. 223–239.

———, *Karl Marx's Theory of History: A Defence*, Princeton University Press, Princeton, 1978.

———, "On the Currency of Egalitarian Justice", *Ethics*, no. 99, July 1989, pp. 906–944.

CONPROGRESA (Coordinación Nacional del Programa de Educación, Salud y Alimentación), *Lineamientos generales para la operación del Programa de Educación, Salud y Alimentación*, CONPROGRESA, Mexico City, 1999.

Constitución Política de los Estados Unidos Mexicanos, Porrúa, Mexico City, 1997.

Cordera, Rolando, "PROGRESA y la experiencia mexicana contra la pobreza. Notas sobre el contexto social y el registro histórico", in *Alivio a la pobreza*, CIESAS/PROGRESA, Mexico City, 1998, pp. 13–23.

Cossío, José Ramón, "Los derechos sociales como normas programáticas y la comprensión política de la Constitución", in Emilio O. Rabasa (coord.), *Ochenta años de la vida constitucional en México*, Cámara de Diputados, LVII Legislatura, Comité de Biblioteca e Informática, Mexico City, 1998, pp. 295–328.

Dasgupta, Partha, *An Inquiry into Well-Being and Destitution*, Clarendon Press, Oxford, 1996.

———, "Environmental and Resource Economics in the World of the Poor", lecture delivered on the forty-fifth anniversary of *Resources for the future*, Resources for the Future, Washington, D.C., 1997, pp. 1–32.

Dieterlen, Paulette, "Algunos aspectos filosóficos del Programa de Educación, Salud y Alimentación", in *Estudios Sociológicos*, vol. XVIII, no. 52, January–April 2000, pp. 191–202.

———,"Democracia, pobreza y exclusión", in Luis Villoro (ed.), *Perspectivas de la democracia en México*, El Colegio Nacional, Mexico City, 2001, pp. 121–174.

———, "Derechos, necesidades básicas y obligación institucional", in Alicia Ziccardi (ed.), *Pobreza, desigualdad social y ciudadanía. Los límites de las políticas sociales en América Latina*, CLACSO, Buenos Aires, 2001, pp. 13–22.

———, "Dos conceptos de pobreza", in Juliana González (coord.), *Moral y poder*, Secretaría de Educación Pública/Academia Mexicana de Ciencias/Consejo Nacional de Ciencia y Tecnología/ Consejo Consultivo de Ciencias de la Presidencia de la República, Mexico City, 2000, pp. 91–98.

———, "La negociación y el acuerdo: dos interpretaciones económicas de la justicia", in *Isegoría*, no. 18, May 1998, pp. 213–222.

———, "PROGRESA y la atención a las necesidades básicas", in *Alivio a la pobreza, análisis del Programa de Educación, Salud y Alimentación*, Mexico City, CIESAS/PROGRESA, 1998, pp. 130–143.

———, "Some Philosophical Considerations on Mexico's Educational, Health, and Food Program", in Arleen L.F. Salles and María Julia Bertomeu (eds.), *Bioethics. Latin American Perspectives*, Rodopi, Amsterdam/Nueva York, 2001, pp. 85–106.

Doyal, Len, "A Theory of Human Need", in G. Brock (ed.), *Necessary Goods. Our Responsibilities to Meet Others' Needs*, pp. 157–172.

Dworkin, Gerald, "Paternalism", *The Monist*, vol. 56, no. 1, January 1972, pp. 64–84.

Dworkin, Ronald, "Do Liberty and Equality Conflict?", in Paul Barker (ed.), *Living as Equals*, Oxford University Press, Oxford, 1996, pp. 23–57.

———, "Liberalism", in S. Hampshire, T.M. Scanlon *et al.*, *Public and Private Morality*, Cambridge University Press, Cambridge, 1980, pp. 113–143.

———, "What Is Equality?, Part 1. Equality of Welfare", *Philosophy and Public Affairs*, vol. 10, no. 3, 1981, pp. 196–204.

Dworkin, Ronald, "What Is Equality?, Part 2. Equality of Resources", *Philosophy and Public Affairs*, vol. 10, no. 4, 1981, pp. 283–345.

———, "Why Liberals Should Care about Equality", *A Matter of Principle*, Harvard University Press, Cambridge, 1985, pp. 205–213.

Elster, Jon, *Alchemies of the Mind*, Cambridge University Press, Cambridge, 1999.

———, "Introduction", *Rational Choice*, Blackwell, Oxford, 1986, pp. 1–33.

———, *Local Justice*, Cambridge University Press, Cambridge, 1994.

———, *The Cement of Society*, Cambridge University Press, Cambridge, 1991.

Estrada Martínez, Rosa Isabel, *El problema de las expulsiones en las comunidades de los altos de Chiapas y los derechos humanos*, Comisión Nacional de Derechos Humanos, Mexico City, 1995.

Feinberg, Joel, *Social Philosophy*, Prentice Hall, New Jersey, 1979.

Foot, Philippa, "The Problem of Abortion and the Doctrine of Double Effect", *Virtues and Vices*, pp. 19–32

———, *Virtues and Vices*, Blackwell, Oxford, 1981.

Gargarella, Roberto, *Las teorías de la justicia después de Rawls*, Paidós, Barcelona, 1999.

Glover, Jonathan, *Causing Death and Saving Lives*, Penguin Books, Harmondsworth, 1981.

Gómez de León, José, Daniel Hernández y Gabriela Vázquez, "El Programa de Educación, Salud y Alimentación: orientaciones y componentes", in PROGRESA, *Más oportunidades para las familias pobres. Evaluación de Resultados del Programa de Educación, Salud y Alimentación. Primeros avances 1999*, Secretaría de Desarrollo Social, Mexico City, 1999, pp. 1–31.

Gómez de León, José, and Paulette Dieterlen, "Diversidad humana, libertad y capacidades en la obra de Amartya Sen", *Metapolítica*, no. 10, vol. 3, April–June 1999, pp. 339–351.

Gómez de León, José, and Susan Parker, "Bienestar y jefatura femenina en los hogares mexicanos", in María de la Paz López and Vania Salles (eds.), *Familia, género y pobreza*, Gimtrap and Miguel Ángel Porrúa, Mexico City, 2000, pp. 11–46.

Gordon, David, and Paul Spicker, *The International Glossary on Poverty*, Zed Books, London/New York, 1999.

Gordon, Sara, "Poverty and social exclusion in Mexico", International Labor Organization Discussion Paper No. 93, 1997. (Another version of this article can be found in "Pobreza, y patrones de exclusión in México", in R. Menjívar, D. Kruijt and L. van Vucht Tijssen (eds.), *Pobreza, exclusión y política social*, UNESCO/FLACSO/University of Utrecht, 1997, pp. 419–445.)

Griffin, James, *Well-Being. Its Meaning, Measurement and Moral Importance*, Clarendon Press, Oxford, 1988.

Hahn, F., and M. Hollis, *Philosophy and Economic Theory*, Oxford University Press, Oxford, 1979, pp. 87–109.

Hart, H.L.A., *The Concept of Law*, Clarendon Law Series, Oxford University Press, Oxford (2nd ed.), 1994.

Hayek, F.A., *The Constitution of Liberty*, The University of Chicago Press, Chicago, 1978.

Heller, Agnes, *The Theory of Needs in Marx*, Allison and Busby, London, 1974.

Heritage, John C., "Ethnomethodology", in Anthony Giddens, Jonathan Turner *et al.*, *Social Theory Today*, Polity Press/Blackwell, Cambridge/Oxford, 1987, pp. 290–350.

Hernández Laos, Enrique, "Retos para la medición de la pobreza en México", paper delivered at the International Symposium on Poverty: Concepts and Methodologies (*Pobreza: conceptos y metodologías*), held in Mexico City on March 28–29, 2001.

Hollis, Martin, "Rational Man and the Social Sciences", in Ross Harrison (ed.), *Rational Action. Studies in Philosophy and Social Science*, Cambridge University Press, Cambridge, 1979, pp. 1–16.

Kant, Immanuel, *Groundwork of the Metaphysic of Morals*, tr. H.J. Paten, New York, Harper Torchbooks, 1964.

Kelley, David, *A Life of One's Own*, CATO Institute, Washington, 1998.

Korsgaard, Christine, *Creating the Kingdom of Ends*, Cambridge University Press, Cambridge, 1996.

Le Grand, Julian, "Equity as an Economic Objective", in B. Almond and D. Hill (eds.), *Applied Philosophy. Morals and Metaphysics in Contemporary Debate*, pp. 183–195.

Levy, Santiago, "La pobreza en México", in Félix Vélez (ed.), *La pobreza en México. Causas y políticas para combatirla*, ITAM/Fondo de Cultura Económica, Mexico City, 1994, pp. 15–112.

———, "La pobreza extrema en México: una propuesta de política", *Estudios Económicos*, vol. 6, no. 1, 1991, pp. 69–73.

Lustig, Nora, "Reflexiones sobre las características del Programa PROGRESA", in *Alivio a la pobreza. Análisis del Programa de Educación, Salud y Alimentación dentro de la política social: Memoria del Seminario*, CIESAS/PROGRESA, Mexico City, 1998, pp. 120–129.

Margalit, Avishai, *The Decent Society*, Harvard University Press, Cambridge, Mass., 1996.

Mas-Colell, Andreu, Michael D. Whinston and Jerry R. Green, *Microeconomic Theory*, Oxford University Press, Oxford, 1995.

Nagel, Thomas, "Equality", *Mortal Questions*, Cambridge University Press, Cambridge, 1980, pp. 106–129.

———, *Equality and Partiality*, Oxford University Press, Oxford, 1991.

———, *The Possibility of Altruism*, Princeton University Press, Princeton, 1978.

Nahmad, Salomón, Tania Carrasco and Sergio Sarmiento, "Acercamiento etnográfico y cultural sobre el impacto del Programa PROGRESA en doce comunidades de seis estados de la República", in *Alivio a la pobreza*, CIESAS/PROGRESA, Mexico City, 1998, pp. 62–109.

Nino, Carlos S., "Sobre los derechos sociales", in M. Carbonell, J.A. Cruz Parcero and R. Vázquez (eds.), *Derechos sociales y derechos de las minorías*, pp. 137–146.

Nozick, Robert, *Anarchy, State, and Utopia*, Basic Books, New York, 1974.

Nussbaum, Martha, "Aristotelian Social Democracy", in G. Brock, *Necessary Goods. Our Responsibilities to Meet Others' Needs*, pp. 135–156.

———, "Capacidades humanas y justicia social. Una defensa del esencialismo aristotélico", in J. Riechman (ed.), *Necesitar, desear, vivir. Sobre necesidades, desarrollo humano, crecimiento económico y sustentabilidad*, pp. 43–104.

Nussbaum, Martha and Amartya Sen (eds.), *The Quality of Life*, Oxford University Press, Oxford, 1993.

O'Neill, Onora, *Faces of Hunger. An Essay on Poverty, Justice and Development*, Allen and Unwin, London, 1986.

———, "Rights, Obligations and Needs", in G. Brock (ed.), *Necessary goods. Our Responsibilities to Meet Others' Needs*, pp. 95–112.

O'Neill, Onora, *Toward Justice and Virtue*, Cambridge University Press, Cambridge, 1998.

Platts, Mark, *Moral Realities. An Essay in Philosophical Psychology*, Routledge, London, 1991.

———, *Sobre usos y abusos de la moral. Ética, sida, sociedad*, Paidós/Instituto de Investigaciones Filosóficas-UNAM, Mexico City, 1999.

Prieto Sanchís, Luis, "Los derechos sociales y el principio de igualdad", in M. Carbonell, J.A. Cruz Parcero and R. Vázquez (eds.), *Derechos sociales y derechos de las minorías*, pp. 15–66.

PROGRESA. Más oportunidades para las familias pobres. Evaluación de Resultados del Programa de Educación, Salud y alimentación. Primeros avances 1999. Secretaría de Desarrollo Social, Mexico City, 1999.

Quinton, A. (ed.), *Political Philosophy*, Oxford University Press, Oxford, 1978, pp. 141–152.

Rakowski, Eric, *Equal Justice*, Oxford University Press, Oxford, 1993.

Rawls, John, *A Theory of Justice*, Harvard University Press, Cambridge, Mass., 1971.

———, *Collected Papers*, ed. Samuel Freeman, Harvard University Press, Cambridge, 1999.

———, "Reply to Alexander and Musgrave", in *Collected Papers*, pp. 232–253.

———, "Social Unity and Primary Goods", in *Collected Papers*, pp. 359–387.

Ray, Debraj, *Development Economics*, Princeton University Press, Princeton, 1998.

Riechman, Jorge, "Necesidades: algunas delimitaciones en las que acaso podríamos convenir", in J. Riechman (coord.), *Necesitar, desear y vivir. Sobre necesidades, desarrollo humano, crecimiento económico y sustentabilidad*, pp. 11–42.

Riechman, Jorge, *Necesitar, desear y vivir. Sobre necesidades, desarrollo humano, crecimiento económico y sustentabilidad*, Los Libros de la Catarata, Madrid, 1998.

Roemer, John, *Equality of Opportunity*, Harvard University Press, Harvard, 1990.

Rousseau, Jean-Jacques, *The Social Contract and Discourses*, Everyman's Library, Dent, London, 1973.

Salcedo, Damián, "Introducción", in A. Sen, *Bienestar, justicia y mercado*, pp. 9–38.

Secretaría de Desarrollo Social, *Mexico's New Social Policy*, paper presented at the OECD, Mexico City, n/d.

Sen, Amartya, *Bienestar, justicia y mercado*, tr. Damián Salcedo, Paidós, Barcelona, 1997.

―――, "Capability and Well-Being", in M. Nussbaum and A. Sen (eds.), *The Quality of Life*, Oxford University Press, Oxford, 1993, pp. 30–53.

―――, "Description as Choice", *Choice, Welfare and Measurement*, Blackwell, Oxford, 1982.

―――, "Equality of What?" in J. Rawls, A. Sen *et al.*, *Liberty, Equality and Law*, University of Utah Press, Salt Lake City, 1987, pp. 139–162.

―――, "La razón antes que la identidad", *Letras Libres*, II, no. 23, November 2000, pp. 14–18 (Spanish version of *Reason Before Identity: The Romanes Lectures, Oxford, 1998*, Oxford University Press, 1999).

―――, *On Economic Inequality*, Clarendon Press, Oxford, 1997.

―――, "Poor, Relatively Speaking", *Resources, Values and Development*, Harvard University Press, Cambridge, 1984.

―――, "Rational Fools", in F. Hahn and M. Hollis, *Philosophy and Economic Theory*, pp. 87–109.

―――, "Rights and Capabilities", in Ted Honderich (ed.), *Morality and Objectivity*, Routledge and Kegan Paul, London, 1985, pp. 130–148.

―――, *Ethics and Economics*, Blackwell, Oxford, 1991.

―――, "The Political Economy of Targeting", in Dominique van de Walle and Kimberly Nead (eds.), *Public Spending and the Poor. Theory and Evidence*, The World Bank/The Johns Hopkins University Press, Baltimore/London, 1995, pp. 11–23.

Sen, Amartya, "The Standard of Living", *The Standard of Living*, ed. Geoffrey Hawthorn, Cambridge University Press, Cambridge, 1990, pp. 1–38.

Singer, Peter, *Practical Ethics*, 2nd. ed., Cambridge University Press, Cambridge, 1994.

Skillen, Anthony, "Welfare State versus Welfare Society?", in B. Almond and D. Hill (eds.), *Applied Philosophy. Moral and Metaphysics in Contemporary Debate*, pp. 202–216.

Skoufias, E., B. Davis and J. Behrman, "Evaluación del sistema de selección de familias beneficiarias en PROGRESA", in *Más oportunidades para las familias pobres*, PROGRESA, Mexico City, 1999, pp. 81–104.

Slack, Paul, *The English Poor Law. 1531–1782*, Cambridge University Press, Cambridge, 1995.

Stigler, G.J., *El economista como predicador y otros ensayos*, tr. Jorge Pascual, Folio, Barcelona, 1987 (2 vols.).

Tamayo, Rolando, "Ensayo preliminar", in H.L.A. Hart, *Postscriptum al concepto de derecho*, Instituto de Investigaciones Jurídicas-UNAM, Mexico City, 2000, pp. XI–XXV.

Vélez, Félix, "Introducción", in F. Vélez (ed.), *La pobreza en México. Causas y políticas para combatirla*, pp. 7–13.

———, (ed.), *La pobreza en México. Causas y políticas para combatirla*, ITAM/Fondo de Cultura Económica, Mexico City, 1994.

Villoro, Luis, *El poder y el valor. Fundamentos de una ética política*, El Colegio de México/Fondo de Cultura Económica, Mexico City, 1997.

Wagstaff, A., E. van Doorslaer y F. Rutten, "Introduction", in *Equity in the Finance and Delivery of Health Care. An International Perspective*, Oxford Medical Publications, Oxford, 1993.

Waldron, Jeremy, *Liberal Rights*, Cambridge University Press, Cambridge, 1993.

Walzer, Michael, *Spheres of Jusitce*, Martin Robertson, Oxford, 1983.

———, "Pluralism: A Political Perspective", in W. Kymlicka (ed.), *The Rights of Minority Cultures*, Oxford University Press, Oxford, 1996, pp. 139–154.

Wiggins, David, "Claims of Needs", in Ted Honderich (ed.), *Morality and Objectivity*, Routledge and Kegan Paul, London, 1985, pp. 149–201.

Williams, Bernard, "The Idea of Equality", *Problems of the Self*, Cambridge University Press, Cambridge, 1979.

———, "The Standard of Living: Interests and Capabilities", in A. Sen, *The Standard of Living*, pp. 94–102.